ROBERT BURNS

His Life, Work and Fame

Robert Burns, the most famous of Scottish poets and the greatest maker and preserver of Scottish songs, was born here on 25 January, 1759.

ROBERT BURNS: HIS LIFE AND WORK

Burns's life.

Robert was the eldest of seven children of William Burnes, a market-gardener from Kincardineshire, and Agnes Brown, from the neighbouring parish of Kirkoswald. William Burnes (his children dropped the 'e' from the name) acquired $7\frac{1}{2}$ acres of land, of which the Burns Monument Trustees still hold six, and with his own hands built on it this cottage of whitewashed clay walls.

When Robert was seven his father rented a small farm $1\frac{1}{2}$ miles away at Mount Oliphant and the family moved there. Robert grew up to a life of toil, hardship and poverty. But Burnes saw to it that his sons were well educated. Robert read all the books he could and developed a remarkable command of literary English. The other great influence on him was folk-song. His mother knew and sang many old songs, though she could not read.

In 1777 the family moved to Lochlea farm, near Tarbolton, where William Burnes died worn out early in 1784. Robert and his brother Gilbert rented the farm of Mossgiel, near Mauchline, and struggled on. Robert became an enthusiastic Freemason.

He had already written many songs and in 1785 began writing satires and "epistles" which, handed about in copies, won him a local celebrity. A love affair with a Mauchline girl, Jean Armour, who later bore him twins, landed him in trouble. Under threat of prosecution by her father, and hard pressed for money, he gave up his share of Mossgiel to Gilbert and planned to emigrate to Jamaica; he decided to print his poems in Kilmarnock to raise funds for the voyage.

The Kilmarnock edition (1786), of which an original copy is shown in the museum here, was enthusiastically received, and praised in the Edinburgh magazines. Burns gave up emigration, went to Edinburgh to publish a second edition, and was lionised there. In 1787—8 he was briefly entangled with an Edinburgh lady, Mrs. MacLehose ("Clarinda"). But he married Jean Armour; it was a happy marriage and they had several children.

Burns wanted to give up farming, but his Edinburgh friends could find him nothing better than a minor post in the Excise in Dumfriesshire, and he had to take another farm there, Ellisland, in 1788. He proved a good officer, was promoted twice and in 1791 gave up Ellisland and moved into Dumfries. He published a revised third edition of his poems in Edinburgh (1793) and died in Dumfries on 21 July, 1796, of heart disease (endocarditis) induced by the rheumatic fever he had suffered in his early years. He lived to be only 37.

Burns's works.

Burns's first love was song. He had a keen musical ear and a great feeling for rhythm. His first poems were songs, the earliest written when he was 15, and on his own evidence he never composed a song without first having a tune in his head. While in Edinburgh he met two music publishers, James Johnson and George Thomson, to  whose collections of Scots songs he was contributing right up to his death; in this field his Dumfriesshire years were specially fruitful. Burns is our first and greatest collector of folk-songs. He rescued some 360, polishing old words or writing new ones.

The second important part of his work is the epistles and satires, their style modelled on that of two earlier Scots poets, Allan Ramsay and Robert Fergusson. These show him as an acute observer and critic of human conduct, with a warm heart, a strong sense of humour and a hatred of hypocrisy. His philosophy of the brotherhood of man was partly inspired by the ideals of Freemasonry. Some of this work is of universal appeal; but much of it, to be really appreciated, needs some knowledge of Burns's 18th century world.

Thirdly, there is **Tam o' Shanter**. "Burns wrote only one tale in verse, but it is the best since Chaucer" (John Buchan). It is a story of witchcraft with comic touches, based on folk-tales Burns heard in his childhood and closely linked with Alloway landmarks still to be seen, the ruined church (Kirk Alloway), the ancient bridge (Brig o' Doon), and the cairn.

Lastly there are Burns's letters, notable for their style and polish, of which over 700 survive.

Examples of all these are shown among the original manuscripts in the museum.

Burns's character and fame.

In Scotland, Burns is more than a literary figure—a popular hero, whose birthday is celebrated by Scots all over the world. He sprang from the country people and their traditions and his undoubted genius owed nothing to fortune. From the beginning his published work was enjoyed by all classes, not only his best but much that is really second-rate. His birthplace has always been venerated, but it became an alehouse before 1800, and remained so till 1880 when it was acquired and restored by the Burns Monument Trustees. The Monument near the Brig o' Doon was planned in 1814 and completed in 1823.

Burns's character was not a complicated one; but it has been variously distorted by both admirers and detractors. His early biographers asserted that he drank to excess: in fact he was an abstemious man. He left several natural children, from the eldest of whom his only surviving posterity is descended; but he was a good husband and father, companion and friend, and a man of religious faith and undaunted courage in many adversities.

" Advertiser Office," Ayr.

CONTENTS

Introduction

Acknowledgements

Cover Picture — Kirk Alloway

INTRODUCTION

Throughout the world, Ayrshire is known as The Land of Burns. It is where the poet was born, grew to manhood and developed from a country lad with rhyming ability to a man of poetic genius.

For the tourist, the county has many places of interest associated with the poet and for the scholar it is a Mecca demanding a pilgrimage.

To understand any man we must know something of his environment and so it is for Robert Burns. In his poem, *The Vision*, he told us that the mantle of his Muse, Coila, is patterned with many vistas of her native shire. To be attuned to Burns we must be familiar with Coila's mantle; a walk by the River Ayr at Barskimming can do more than a visit to a museum.

In recent years, much has been done to stimulate the interest of the vast number of visitors to the Burns Country but we must ensure that in a county full of Burns-Lore we do not concentrate on a few places of interest and neglect many others deserving of attention. Neither must we allow the tartan and tea towels to take over from the real associations with Burns.

Often, even Ayrshire people are not aware that places well known to them have associations with the poet and guided tours of the area unwittingly neglect locations of much more interest and importance in the Burns story than the museums and restored houses they visit. The guide book does not deserve to be printed that takes us to Lochlea without drawing our attention to Boghead, Adamhill, Littlehill and Coldcothill, or directs us to the many attractions of Mauchline without reference to Armour's House, Richmond's House or Bridge Holm.

Unfortunately, much of the information on the less publicised associations with the poet can be obtained only by lengthy research through sources which are not readily available. Even then, the researcher without wide local knowledge of Ayrshire is at a great disadvantage.

There has been a need for the extensive Burns-Lore of Ayrshire to be collated and that has been the aim in the preparation of this book. Places in Ayrshire directly associated with the poet, referred to in his works, or associated with his friends are listed alphabetically; for each, its location is described and its connection with the poet explained.

Though the list of locations is comprehensive, this is not a concordance to the works of Burns and the references from the poems and letters quoted for any location are not necessarily complete.

Every location has been described fully and positive identification should be easy. Except for towns and villages, and where exact locations can not be traced, map references have been given; these should seldom be required but they have been included to avoid any possible difficulty. The map references relate to the Ordnance Survey Map (1: 50,000 Series) and are covered by Sheets, 63, 64, 70, 71, 76, 77 and 78.

To help the reader to visualise locations where buildings are no longer extant and street plans have altered, sketches have been included of the approximate street plans of the main towns and villages as they were at the time of Burns. With a few exceptions, only locations referred to in the text are included in the plans.

The reader who is not knowledgeable about the poet, may wonder at the spellings of the family surname. The poet's father, William Burnes, always used the east of Scotland spelling of his forebears, and the family followed suit with Burnes or Burness during most of his lifetime. As early as July 1780 the poet used the Ayrshire spelling, Burns, and after their father's death in 1784, Robert and his brother Gilbert began to drop the 'e' and 'ss' from their surname by habit. We can speculate that if Robert's poems had been published before his father's death, out of deference to his esteemed parent, our National Bard might have been known to the world as Robert Burnes or Burness.

Writers on local history have been accused of debasing their work by amassing all of the facts they can discover with no criterion for distinguishing the trivial from the significant. This writer pleads guilty to having brought together, not only the trivial and the significant but also fact and fable claim and counter-claim. No apology is made for having done so as all of the information included is now part of Ayrshire Burns-Lore. Almost 200 years after the poet's death, a record of only indisputable facts about Burns would be short indeed. In any case, the bare facts alone can be obtained easily, whereas much of the information and many of the anecdotes are now obscure, neglected and in danger of being lost. As often as possible, an indication is given of what can and can not be proved.

This book will have achieved the aim of its author if its factual information assists the researcher into Burns, if the anecdotes stimulate the interest of the more casual enquirer, and if, in any way, it helps to perpetuate the memory of Robert Burns.

Troon :
November 1985

ACKNOWLEDGEMENTS

I am indebted to many people for the assistance they have given me as I have collected the Burns-Lore of Ayrshire. Some were already friends — many with a shared interest in Burns — and many others have become friends.

It would be impracticable for me to name everyone who has helped me and, for the majority, I must hope that my gratitude was obvious to them.

I must express my special thanks to a few: to Sam Hay, Curator of the Bachelors' Club, Tarbolton for being generous to me with both his time and knowledge of Burns in Tarbolton parish: to John Loudon, Prestwick and Joan Mitchell, Glasgow for assistance with the preparation of my manuscript; and to the staff of the Carnegie Reference Library, Ayr — it is doubtful if the work could have been completed without ready access to the library's collection and the helpful attitude of its staff.

I wish to record my thanks to the following persons for their authority to reproduce photographs from books and photographic collections :
Baroness Elliot of Harwood for the book *Tennant's Stalk* by her sister, Nancy, Lady Crathorne; Mr. J.D.S.McMillan, Mauchline for the book *Mauchline — Town and Country* by J.Taylor Gibb; Mr. J. Weir, Catrine for his history of Lodge St. James Tarbolton Kilwinning No. 135; Mr. and Mrs. R. Campbell, Irvine for their Irvine collection; Kyle and Carrick District Council for the Carnegie Library collection; and Kilmarnock and Loudoun District Council for the Dick Institute collection and their Kilmarnock brochure. I also acknowledge having reproduced photographs from the Rev. James Muir's book *Burns to His 17th Year*. All of the new photographs were taken by my daughter, Fiona Balish.

A.M.B.

The AYRSHIRE
BOOK OF
BURNS–LORE

DEDICATED
TO
MY WIFE, LILIAS
AND DAUGHTER, FIONA

who have borne with me while I
searched through cemeteries,
meandered around museums, and
buried myself in Burns books

'That I for poor auld Scotland's sake
Some usefu' plan or book could make
Or sing a sang at least.'
BURNS

The AYRSHIRE BOOK OF BURNS-LORE

A. M. BOYLE

Alloway Publishing
AYR

© ANDREW M. BOYLE

First Published in 1985
by
Alloway Publishing Ltd.,
Ayr.

Reprinted 1986

Printed in Scotland
by
Walker & Connell Ltd.,
Hastings Square, Darvel,
Ayrshire.

ISBN 0-907526-18-7

Year	Occurrence	Reference
1732—Agnes Broun, the poet's mother, born on 15 March (Died 14 January, 1820)		Whitestone Cottage Craigenton Farm
1744—Agnes Broun moved into Maybole to live with her maternal grandmother.		Maybole
1750—William Burnes, the poet's father, moved from the east of Scotland to Dundonald, Ayrshire		Fairlie House
1752—William Burnes moved to Alloway		Doonside, Doonholm Doonside Mill
1756—William Burnes and Agnes Broun met at Maybole Fair		Maybole
1757—William Burnes constructed the cottage at Alloway. William and Agnes married at Maybole on 15 December		Burns Cottage New Gardens
1759– Robert Burn(e)s born in the cottage on 25 January (Died 21 July, 1796)		Burns Cottage New Gardens
1760—Gilbert Burn(e)s born in the cottage on 28 September (Died 8 April, 1827)		Lochlea Farm, Mossgiel Farm, Kilmarnock
1762 –Agnes Burn(e)s born in the cottage on 30 September (Died 17 October, 1834)		
1764—Annabella Burn(e)s born at the cottage on 14 November (Died 2 March, 1832)		Tarbolton
1765—Robert and Gilbert attended school at Alloway Mill under Mr. Campbell. Campbell left and William Burnes joined other parents in employing John Murdoch to conduct a school at Alloway.		Alloway Mill Simpson's Inn Murdoch's House
1766—William Burnes rented Mount Oliphant Farm and the family moved in at Whitsun		Mount Oliphant Farm
1767—William Burnes, Jnr., born at Mount Oliphant on 30 July. (Died 24 July, 1790).		Murdoch's House
1769—John Burnes born at Mount Oliphant on 12 July (Died 4 December, 1783)		
1771—Isabella Burn(e)s born at Mount Oliphant on 27 June (Died 4 December, 1858).		Bridge House Kirk-Alloway
1772—Robert and Gilbert attended Dalrymple School		Dalrymple
1773—Robert attended Ayr Grammar School under John Murdoch. Robert composed his first published song, Handsome Nell.		Ayr Grammar School Murdoch's House Purclewan Mill
1775—Robert attended Hugh Rodger's School at Kirkoswald and met Peggy Thomson		Kirkoswald Rodger's School Ballochneil Farm Peggy Thomson's House,
1777—William Burnes rented Lochlea Farm and the family moved in at Whitsun.		Lochlea Farm
1779—Robert joined Tarbolton dancing class against his father's wishes		Lochlea Farm Tarbolton

1780—Robert and Gilbert, together with five other young men founded the Bachelors' Club, Tarbolton

Bachelors' Club
Tarbolton

1781—Robert courted and proposed marriage to Alison (Ellison) Begbie who rejected him. He was initiated into Lodge St. David Tarbolton on 4 July and moved to Irvine to learn flax dressing in mid-summer. Dispute started between William Burnes and his landlord.

Carnell House
Bachelors' Club
Freemasonry, Irvine,
Glasgow Vennel,
Lochlea Farm
Old Place Farm

1782—Irvine flax dressing workshop destroyed by fire. Robert worked in other premises and then returned to Lochlea in March. In July he left Lodge St. David for Lodge St. James Tarbolton.

Irvine,
Glasgow Vennel
Freemasonry

1783—Robert won £3 prize for flax dressing at Lochlea. Robert and Gilbert arranged with Gavin Hamilton to rent Mossgiel Farm. Robert started his first Commonplace Book. Dispute between William Burnes and his landlord found mainly in favour of Burnes.

Lochlea Farm
Mossgiel Farm

Shawwood

1784—William Burnes died at Lochlea on 13 February and was buried at Alloway. The Burnes family moved into Mossgiel in March. Robert became Depute Master of Lodge St. James, Tarbolton.

Lochlea Farm
Mossgiel Farm
Alloway Kirkyard
Freemasonry

1785—Elizabeth Paton gave birth to an illegitimate child (Elizabeth Burns) on 22 May. Robert met Jean Armour in Mauchline. First Commonplace Book finished.

Largieside
Mauchline, Mauchline
Bleaching Green

1786—Jean Armour pregnant by Robert; her parents opposed to her common-law marriage to Robert and sent her to Paisley. Robert courted Highland Mary and made plans to emigrate to Jamaica. Kilmarnock Edition of Robert's work published on 31 July. Jean Armour gave birth to twins on 3 September. Mary Campbell died at Greenock in October. Robert abandoned plans to emigrate and on 27 November left Mauchline for his first visit to Edinburgh.

Kilmarnock
Failford
Stairaird
Old Rome
Garallan

1787—Robert returned to Mauchline in June amid national acclaim. Jean and Robert's infant daughter, Jean, died during October. Robert and Jean met again and Jean became pregnant. Robert returned to Edinburgh and went on tours of the Highlands and Stirlingshire.

Mauchline
Kirkyard,
Willie's Mill

1788—Robert returned to Mauchline during February. He found Jean lodging at Willie's Mill, took her to a house in Mauchline and they began married life together. Jean gave birth to twins on 3 March and both died within days. Robert received Excise instruction at Mauchline and Tarbolton. He took over Ellisland Farm, Dumfries on 11 June, leaving Jean at Mauchline while he built a house In December Jean joined Robert at Isle, Dumfries

Willie's Mill
Back Causeway
Mauchline Kirkyard
Beechgrove Cottage
Gavin Hamilton's
House,
Morton's Ballroom,
Ronald's Inn

1789—Robert attended Gilbert's wedding to Jean Breckenridge of Kilmarnock on 21 June and paid a visit to Mrs. Dunlop at Dunlop House before returning home.

Dunlop House
Kilmarnock

1798— Gilbert Burns gave up Mossgiel and moved to Dinning, Nithsdale. His mother moved with him and the family of William and Agnes Burnes ended their connection with Ayrshire for several years. About 1843 the poet's youngest sister, Isabella Burns Begg returned to live at Bridge House, Alloway until her death in 1858.

Bridge House

Kirk Alloway

ACHMACHALLA

It is referred to in the poem *HALLOWE'EN* - *'He sin gat Eppie Sim wi' wean, That lived in Achmachalla.'* According to the Rev. James Muir, Minister of Kirkoswald, in his book, Burns To His Seventeenth Year, Achmachalla was a fictitious name for a dwelling called Fardincalla on the lands of Kirklands Farm, Kirkoswald, a half mile south of the village. The exact location cannot be traced.

ADAMHILL FARM   Map Ref. 430 304

Situated on the south side on the A719 Ayr/Galston Road, one mile east of the B730 Dundonald/Tarbolton Road. It is a neighbouring farm to Lochlea and was the home of the poet's friend, John Rankine and his daughter Anne. John Rankine was addressed in the poems *EPISTLE TO JOHN RANKINE* and *EPITAPH ON JOHN RANKINE.* In Burns lore he is known as *'rough, rude, ready-witted Rankine,'* as quoted from the Epistle. Late in life, Rankine moved from Adamhill to Galston where he lived in Old Manse Close. He died on 2 February, 1810 and is buried in Galston Kirkyard.

Anne Rankine, the daughter, was the same age as Burns and claimed to be *'Annie',* the heroine of the song *THE RIGS OF BARLEY.* She said that she had expressed surprise to the poet at having been mentioned in his poems and that he had replied, - 'Oh, ay! I was just wanting to give you a cast amang the lave (rest).' She married John Merry, Innkeeper, Cumnock, and lived most of her life there. In 1843, she died aged 84 years, and is buried in Cumnock Kirkyard. The poet did not identify the heroine of the song.

In his Reminiscences Of A Long Life (1906), A.B. Todd, Ayrshire poet and antiquarian who was a close friend of Anne Rankine's son, Hugh Merry, gives the following account of an incident at Adamhill as handed down to Merry - 'Tarbolton Kirk Session were informed that the local Assistant Minister, The Rev. John McMath, had got drunk at Adamhill in the company of John Rankine and Robert Burns. The Session arranged to visit the farm to enquire into the incident and Rankine plotted to save McMath. He gave the visitors refreshments which he repeatedly topped up with 'hot water' from a kettle by the fire. Unknown to the visitors he had filled the kettle, not with water, but with whisky. Eventually, when all of the Session were drunk, he had them loaded on to an open cart and dropped off at their homes in Tarbolton, in full view of the public 'There may have been some truth in the allegation against the Rev. McMath as he had to demit his post a few years later for excessive drinking. He was addressed by the poet in the poem *TO THE REV. JOHN McMATH.*

John Rankine's sister, Margaret, was the first wife of John Lapraik, the Muirkirk poet and friend of Burns.

Also see: Cumnock; Galston. Dalfram; Tarbolton.

AFTON LODGE   Map Ref. 416 257

Situated on the north side on the A758 Ayr/Mauchiine Road, one mile east of Mossblown. The house is still inhabited. It was built in 1790 for Mrs Catherine Stewart, formerly of Stair House. She was a daughter of James Gordon of Afton, New Cumnock and the name Afton Lodge arose from this connection.

Mrs Stewart was the first of the upper classes to befriend Burns and encourage him in his writing. In 1791 the poet sent her a collection of 13 manuscripts of his later and then unpublished compositions, including *TAM O'SHANTER* and *SWEET AFTON.* The collection is now known as the Afton Manuscript. In his introduction to the collection, Burns wrote — 'To Mrs General Stewart of Afton — the first person of her sex and rank that patronised his humble lays, this manuscript collection of poems is presented, with the sincerest emotions of grateful respect, by The Author.'

AFTON LODGE

Early biographers of Burns claimed that the song *SWEET AFTON* was composed as a compliment to Mrs Stewart and that the 'Afton' referred to was a burn in the vicinity of Afton Lodge. As it was one of the collection in the Afton Manuscript, it may have been intended as a compliment but the circumstances gave rise to the erroneous claim regarding the river. The poet recorded that the song related to the River Afton, New Cumnock.
Also see: Afton River; Stair House.

AFTON RIVER   Map Ref. 630 050
The river flows north through Glen Afton, New Cumnock and joins the River Nith at the Map Reference shown. It is referred to in the song *SWEET AFTON*.

The poet was familiar with the area and had several friends in Glen Afton. A cairn and picnic area on the west bank of the river commemorate his association with the district.

In a letter to Mrs. Dunlop of Dunlop dated 5 February, 1789, Burns wrote - 'There is a small river, Afton, near New Cumnock.... I intended a compliment.... to Afton as follows' (followed by the song *SWEET AFTON*). When the song was composed, Burns referred to the river as 'Clear Afton'. He later changed 'Clear' to 'Sweet'.

Local legend maintains that the song was written in an inn by the River Afton at New Cumnock. The poet had halted at the inn on his way from Ellisland to Mauchline and had gone to visit Mr. Logan of Laight, Glen Afton, for the evening. During his absence from the inn, the landlady had spread news of the poet's presence, expecting to have a busy, lively night on his return. When Burns returned he appeared to be pre-occupied with his thoughts and went straight to his room. In the morning he sent a servant to Laight with a draft of the song Clear Afton which he had composed on his way back to the inn.

The inn cannot be traced. Local tradition maintains that the existing Castle Hotel was the inn concerned but this cannot be substantiated. About 1900, the inn in which Burns lodged was described as then being a farmhouse on the banks of the River Afton and that does not support the tradition concerning the Castle Hotel which has no history of having been a farmhouse.

Also see: Ashmark; Corsincon; Knockshinnoch; Laight; Pencloe; New Cumnock.

GLEN AFTON
'Flow gently sweet Afton, amang thy green braes.'

AIKENBRAE FARM   Map Ref. 369 272 (approx)

The farm was demolished for the development of Prestwick Airport. It was situated to the south of the A739 Monkton/Tarbolton Road and north of the main runway of the airport. The steading was opposite the location of the present control tower.

The farm was the home of Matthew Paterson and his wife, Ann Ronald, both of whom are buried in Monkton Kirkyard.

Matthew Paterson was friendly with Burns in Tarbolton and was admitted into the Bachelors' Club early in 1782. It is not known where he lived in Tarbolton; members of the Paterson family farmed at Crofthead, Tunnoch and Skeoch in Tarbolton area, at Pant in Stair Parish and at Aikenbrae.

Isabella Burns Begg, the poet's youngest sister, recalled having danced with Matthew Paterson at a Bachelors' Club Ball in Tarbolton. She had been attending a sewing class in the village while her older brothers and sisters attended the ball. Although she was only 11 years old, and waiting to be accompanied home to Lochlea, her sister Annie (Annabella) took her into the ball to partner Matthew Paterson, whose intended partner had let him down.

Ann Ronald was a daughter of William Ronald, Laird of Bennals, Mossblown. She was referred to in the poem *THE RONALDS OF THE BENNALS* — '*Then Anna comes in, the pride of her kin.*' The poet was keen to court Ann but was afraid of being rebuffed because of her family's superior social standing.

Also see: Bachelors' Club; Bennals; Monkton.

AILSA CRAIG
Map Ref. 020 997

A rocky island in the Firth of Clyde, 10 miles west of Girvan. Burns referred to it in the song *DUNCAN GRAY* — '*Meg was deaf as Ailsa Craig.*'

In a letter dated 1788 from Mossgiel, the poet wrote to his maternal uncle, Samuel Broun, Kirkoswald — 'I am impatient to know if the Ailsa fowling be commenced for the season yet as I want 3 or 4 stones of feathers.'

Local tradition maintains that while he was lodging at Ballochneil Farm, Kirkoswald in 1775, and attending Rodger's School in the village, the poet and his friend John Niven went to Ailsa Craig with Douglas Graham of Shanter Farm, the man who was later to be the model for Tam O'Shanter in the poem of that name. It is also said that Graham's boat was called 'The Tam' and that it was from the name of the boat that the poet chose the name Tam for the subject of his poem.

Also see: Ballochneil Farm; Laigh Park Farm; Shanter Farm.

ALLOWAY

Situated on the B7024 Ayr/Maybole Road, 2 miles south of Ayr town centre.

Now within the Burgh of Ayr, Alloway was originally a separate village. It commands a place of honour in the Burns story as the poet's birthplace.

When Burns was a boy in Alloway, Kirk-Alloway was dilapidated but still at least partially roofed. The Old Doon Bridge was the only bridge over the river in the vicinity of the village until he was 13 years of age when his future father-in-law, James Armour, built the bridge at Doonfoot in 1772. The village was only a hamlet but most of the mansion houses on the south bank of the Doon had been built and their grounds laid out.

The main roads in the area were similar to what they are at present. Armstrong's 1775 Map of Ayrshire shows that by then a road existed from Ayr through Alloway and on to Old Doon Bridge, generally on the line of the present B7024 Ayr/Alloway/Maybole Road. Another road is shown from Ayr to Doonfoot and beyond, generally on the line of the A719 Ayr/Dunure Road, over the bridge of 1772.

In 1755/56 the poet's father, William Burnes, had constructed the road now called Greenfield Avenue, which runs parallel to the River Doon and links the roads referred to in the preceding paragraph.

The modern bridge over the River Doon at Alloway was not built until 1815. At that time the road from Kirk-Alloway to the Old Doon Bridge and beyond was re-aligned to cross the new bridge.

Before the road systems described were constructed, the original track from Ayr to Old Doon Bridge and into South Ayrshire, ran to the west of both Burns Cottage and Kirk-Alloway and it was probably existing as a track when the poet was a boy.

The many places of interest associated with the poet in the vicinity are dealt with separately.

Also see: Alloway Mill; Bridge House; Burns Cottage; Doonholm; Doon River; Doonside; Doonside Mill; Greenan Bridge; Greenfield Avenue; Kirk-Alloway; Monuments, etc,; Newark; New Gardens; Old Doon Bridge; Tam O'Shanter's Journey.

ALLOWAY MILL
Map Ref. 324 187

Situated on the north bank of the River Doon, about 300 yards from the mouth of the river. It is still extant but no longer a working mill.

Tradition maintains that about 1755/56, while the poet's father was working at Doonholm, Alloway and before he met his future wife, Agnes Broun, he was attracted by a girl he met regularly at Alloway Mill. He wrote a letter to the girl but placed it in his kist (trunk) rather than give it to her. When he met Agnes he destroyed the letter.

In 1765, when the poet was 6 years of age, he attended a school at Alloway Mill conducted by a William Campbell. The school closed when Campbell left to take up the post as Master of Ayr Workhouse. The building in which the school was held is not known and has probably been demolished.

The school should not be confused with one conducted at Alloway by John Murdoch, later of Ayr Grammar School. Murdoch's school was held in a tenement situated near Burns Cottage and demolished in 1878.

Also see: Ayr Grammar School; John Murdoch's House.

ANNBANK

Situated on the B742 Mossblown/Coylton Road, one mile south of Mossblown.

William Cunningham of Annbank and Enterkine was referred to as 'Annbank' in the poem THE FETE CHAMPETRE — 'Annbank, wha guessed the ladies' taste, He gies a Fete Champetre.'

Also see: Enterkine.

DAMHOUSE OF ARDLOCHAN
circa 1900

ARDLOCHAN

An area at the north end of Maidenhead Bay, a half mile north of Maidens village.

John Niven, blacksmith, designated as from Ardlochan or Damhouse of Ardlochan, is accepted as having been the model of the 'Smith' in the poem TAM O'SHANTER — 'That ev'ry naig was ca'd a shoe on, The smith and thee gat roarin fou on.'

The site of Niven's Smiddy (Smithy) is unknown. At any part of Ardlochan it would have been within a half mile of Shanter Farm, home of Douglas Graham, the model for 'Tam' in the poem TAM O'SHANTER.

Tradition maintains that John Niven was the first blacksmith to introduce a cart with wheels that rotated on a fixed axle. This serves as a reminder that generally at the time of Burns, pack animals or sledges were in use and carts were only being introduced.

John Niven was father of Robert Niven, farmer and miller, Ballochneil, Kirkoswald. Burns lodged at Ballochneil in 1775 while attending school in Kirkoswald. The poet must have known John Niven.
Also see: Ballochneil Farm and Mill; Damhouse of Ardlochan; Maidens; Shanter Farm.

ARMOUR'S HOUSE   Map Ref. 498 273

The parental home of the poet's wife, Jean Armour, until shortly before her marriage, was situated on the west side of Cowgate, Mauchline, about 30 yards south of Loudoun Street. The Whitefoord Arms stood on the west side of the Cowgate/Loudoun Street junction and the Armour house was immediately behind it, separated from it by a narrow lane.

The house was owned by the poet's father-in-law, James Armour, a prosperous master mason and contractor. His standing in the community is illustrated by the Mauchline Church records which show that he rented one of the most expensive pews at a cost of 10/8 per year. He is reputed to have been involved in the building of Dumfries House, Cumnock: Skeldon House. Dalrymple, and numerous bridges throughout Ayrshire. His wife was Mary Smith, daughter of another Mauchline stone mason.
Also see: Cowgate; Greenan Bridge; Whitefoord Arms.

Jean Armour Burns and Grand-daughter

ASHMARK   Map Ref. 611 106

Situated in Glen Afton, New Cumnock, 2 miles south of the town. It was the home of John Murdoch, whose daughter, Mary Murdoch lived with her aunt, Mrs Logan, wife of the poet's friend, John Logan of Laight.

Mary Murdoch has been suggested as the heroine of the song SWEET AFTON — 'My Mary's asleep by thy murmuring stream.' The poet did not identify the heroine. Nothing else is known of Mary Murdoch.

John Murdoch of Ashmark should not be confused with John Murdoch, schoolmaster, who taught Burns at Alloway and Ayr.
Also see: Afton River; Laight; New Cumnock.

ASSLOSS HOUSE   Map Ref: 440 398
    Situated on Assloss Road, Kilmarnock, a half mile south of Glasgow Road,
at a part two miles east of Kilmarnock Town Centre. The house is still occupied.
    It was the home of Major William Parker, fellow mason and friend of Burns.
He was Right Worshipful Master of Lodge St John Kilmarnock No. 24 (now No.
22) when the poet was made an Honorary Member and was referred to in the
Masonic Song composed by Burns for the occasion — *'Ye sons of old Killie,
assembled by Willie.'*
    In a letter dated 8 September, 1786 to Robert Muir, Kilmarnock, the poet
enclosed a copy of the poem *THE CALF* and suggested that it be read to Mr. W.
Parker.
    The poet sent his regards to Messrs. W. and H. Parker in a letter dated 26
August, 1787 to Robert Muir, Kilmarnock. 'H. Parker' was William's brother,
Hugh, a Kilmarnock banker who was himself addressed by Burns in the poem
EPISTLE TO HUGH PARKER.
Also see: Freemasonry; Kilmarnock

AUCHENBAY FARM   Map Ref. 486 235
    Situated on the Ochiltree/Barskimming Road, 2 miles north of Ochiltree.
The farm was the home of John Tennant, second son of John Tennant of
Glenconner. It is reasonable to presume that Burns visited the farm. John Tennant
of Auchenbay was referred to in the poem *EPISTLE TO JAMES TENNANT* —
'An' Auchenbay, I wish him joy.'
    In a letter dated 22 December, 1788, the poet wrote to John Tennant and
thanked him for a case of whisky received. The letter was addressed to Tennant
as c/o Mr. Robb, Innkeeper, Ayr.
    When the Burnes family lived at Mount Oliphant, Alloway the Tennant
family lived at the neighbouring farm of Laigh Corton. During 1773, John
Tennant attended Ayr Grammar School with Burns and both lodged with John
Murdoch, School Master, in his home in Sandgate, Ayr.
    John Tennant of Auchenbay later took over the neighbouring farm of
Steelpark and eventually farmed at Shield Farm, St. Quivox and at Girvan Mains.
Late in life he purchased the lands of Creoch, Ochiltree, then described as 'a
considerable estate.'
Also see: Glenconner Farm; Laigh Corton Farm; Murdoch's House.

AUCHENBLANE   Map Ref. 262 079
    Situated on the east side on the A77 Maybole/Kirkoswald Road, one mile
north of Kirkoswald.
    Ann Gillespie, wife of John Davidson the prototype of Souter Johnie, is
described as having been born at Wester Auchenblane Farm. No farm of that name
exists at present but it was probably part of the present Auchenblane Farm which
is at the Map Reference shown.
    The poet's maternal grandmother died at Craigenton Farm, Turnberry when
his mother, Agnes Broun, was only 10 years of age. Ann Gillespie worked at
Craigenton for 2 years and helped Agnes, who was the eldest of the family, to
look after her 5 brothers and sisters.
Also see: Craigenton Farm; Glenfoot; Souter Johnie's Cottage.

AUCHINCRUIVE   Map Ref. 382 236
    The house and estate are on the south side of the A758 Ayr/Mauchline
Road, one mile east of the A77 Ayr by-pass.
    It was the home of Mrs. Mary Oswald, subject of the poem *ODE SACRED
TO THE MEMORY OF MRS OSWALD OF AUCHINCRUIVE.* In January,
1789, Burns and his horse were settling into an inn in Sanquhar on a wet, stormy
night en route from Ellisland to Mauchline when the funeral cortege of Mrs

Oswald arrived on its way to Auchincruive. The poet had to leave and make his way 11 miles through the storm to the next inn at New Cumnock.

Auchincruive was also the home of Mrs Lucy Oswald. Burns wrote the song *O' WAT YE WHA'S IN YON TOWN* to Jean Lorimer but changed the reference from 'Jeanie' to 'Lucy' and sent a copy of it to Mrs. Lucy Oswald. Before her marriage, Mrs Oswald was Lucy Johnson, and under that name wrote the tune to which Burns set his song *TO MARY IN HEAVEN*.

Lucy Oswald's husband, Richard Oswald, was referred to in the poem *SECOND HERON ELECTION BALLAD* — '*An' there'll be wealthy young Richard.*'

LUCY JOHNSON OSWALD

AUCHINLECK

Situated on the A76 Mauchline/Cumnock Road, 2 miles north of Cumnock. The Rev. John Dun, Minister of Auchinleck, wrote a reply to the poem *ADDRESS TO THE DIEL* in a volume of sermons published in 1790. The publisher was John Wilson, Kilmarnock, who also printed the Kilmarnock edition of our poet's work.

Local tradition maintains that John Murdoch, the school teacher who taught Burns at Alloway and Ayr Grammar School, belonged to Auchinleck where his father was Session Clerk of the Parish Church. This can neither be proved nor disproved.

Also see: Auchinleck House; John Murdoch's House.

AUCHINLECK HOUSE   Map Ref. 507 230

Situated north of the B7036 Auchinleck/Ochiltree Road, one mile west of Auchinleck. The house, which was built in 1780, is still extant but roofless and dilapidated.

It was referred to in a suppressed stanza of the poem *THE VISION* — '*Nearby arose a mansion fine, The seat of many a muse divine.*' In a footnote to the poem, Burns indicated that the reference was to Auchinleck House.

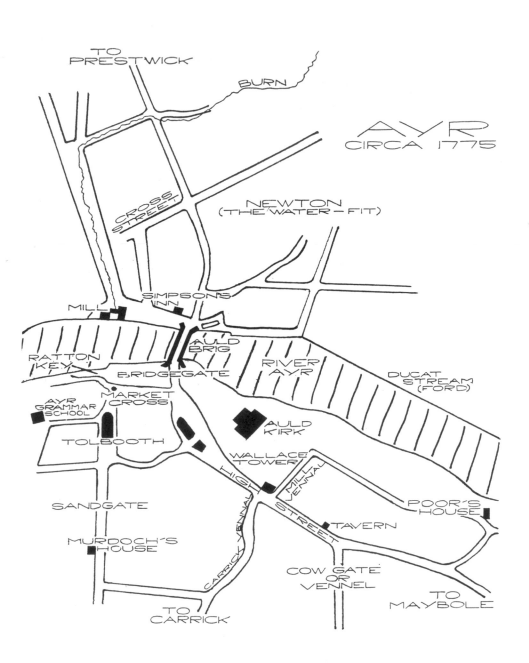

By his reference, the poet intended a compliment to the Boswell family, particularly to his contemporary, James Boswell, famed as the biographer of Doctor Johnson. Burns and Boswell never met although the poet tried to arrange a meeting.

AUCHINSKIETH   Map Ref. 456 337

The mansion house, now called Dallars, is situated 300 yards west of the A76 Kilmarnock/Mauchline Road at Crossroads. It is within 2 miles of the poet's former home at Lochlea Farm. In a note to a suppressed stanza of the poem THE VISION Burns indicated that the following description related to Auchinskeith - '*Where Cessnock pours in gurgling sound.*'

The present house was built in 1779, before the poem was composed. In Armstrong's 1775 Map of Ayrshire it is spelled Auchinskeigh. It is not known when the name was changed to Dollars and subsequently to Dallars.

The Rev. Dr. James Mackinlay, Minister of Laigh Kirk, Kilmarnock, who is referred to in the poem THE ORDINATION, was tutor to the family of Sir William Cunningham at Auchinskieth while he was a probationary minister.

In a letter from Ellisland, dated 16 October, 1789, to Captain Riddell, Dumfries, Burns asked for a letter to be forwarded on his behalf to Sir William Cunningham of Robertland and Auchinskieth.

Also see: Laigh Kirk; Robertland.

AYR

Situated on the Ayrshire coast, at the mouth of the River Ayr. It is an important centre in the Burns Country, indeed, the name is almost synonymous with Burns.

The poet was very familiar with the town of his day and many of its inhabitants. In the Statistical Account of 1775, the population of Ayr Parish was only 2964, compared with Irvine's 4025; it grew during the succeeding 25 years but not to a marked degree; by 1791 the population of the burgh was 3871 and the Parish 4647. As Burns knew it, apart from the Fort and St. John's Church, Ayr consisted of Sandgate, South Harbour Street, High Street to Alloway Street and Mill Street. Alloway Street was the Cow Vennel or Gate and Carrick

AYR FROM THE NORTH
circa 1900

Street was Carrick Vennel. Until 1786 the Auld Brig was the only bridge over the river, and only a few streets had been developed north of the river.

High Street was the market street, badly fouled by the litter and offal of the various trades. The fish, meal and butter markets of today are accurate indications of the original sites. Horses and cattle were sold on open ground now occupied by Burns Statue Square and cattle market.

The poet made numerous references to Ayr, the most famous being in the poem *TAM O'SHANTER* — '*Auld Ayr, whom ne'er a town surpasses, For honest men and bonie lassies.*

The numerous places of interest for their association with Burns are dealt with separately.

Also see: Alloway; Ayr Auld Kirk; Ayr Grammar School; Ayr River; Bridge House; Brigs of Ayr; Burns Cottage; Doonholm House; Doon River; Doonside House; Doonside Mill; Ducat Stream; Greenan Bridge; Kirk-Alloway; Monuments etc; Murdoch's House; Museums, etc; New Gardens; Old Doon Bridge; Park House; Simpson's Inn; Tam O'Shanter's Journey; Wallace Tower; Water-Fit.

AYR AULD KIRK   Map Ref. 339 218

Situated off the east side of High Street, Ayr, and on the south bank of the River Ayr.

The church dates from the 17th century when Oliver Cromwell gave a grant of £600 to the people of Ayr to replace the Church of St John which he had requisitioned.

Robert Burns was baptised in the cottage at Alloway by the Rev. Dr. William Dalrymple, Minister of the Auld Kirk. The poet and his parents were regular attenders at the Kirk until Alloway had a new place of worship to replace 'Kirk-Alloway'.

AYR AULD KIRK
Attended by the poet as a boy.

Rev. Dr. Dalrymple was referred to in the poem *THE TWA HERDS* - *'Dalrymple has been lang our fae.'* He was also referred to in the poem *THE KIRK'S ALARM* as *'Dalrymple mild.'* He was the uncle of the poet's patrons, James Dalrymple of Orangefield and Robert Aiken of Ayr.

A board at the main gate of the kirk shows that the following people associated with the poet are buried in the kirkyard:-

1. Robert Aiken — An Ayr lawyer who was a close friend of the poet. Burns referred to him as his 'first kind patron' and as 'orator Bob.' The poem *THE COTTER'S SATURDAY NIGHT* was dedicated to Aiken. Also see: Whitehill.

2. Provost William Ferguson — A retired medical practioner and Provost of Ayr. He employed tne poet's father, William Burnes as head gardener at Doonholm, Alloway. He also leased Mount Oliphant Farm to William Burnes and lent him £100 to buy stock.

3. Doctor Charles — Described at the gateway as 'A playmate of the poet's boyhood.' Doctor George Charles, was born in 1757 and died on 21 July, 1831 aged 74 years. He was provost of Ayr from 1798 to 1804. When recalling their friends in Ayr. Gilbert Burns wrote — 'Dr Charles of Ayr, who was a little older than my brother, and with whom he had a longer and closer intimacy than with any of the others, which did not, however, continue in after-life.' On writing to William Niven, Maybole from Mossgiel on 30 August, 1786, Burns addressed it c/o Thomas Piper, Surgeon, to be left at Dr Charles's shop, Ayr.

4. John Ballantine — Provost of Ayr and friend and patron of Burns. Also see: Castlehill.

5. Rev. Dr. William McGill — Minister of Ayr. He was referred to in the poem *THE KIRK'S ALARM* as *'Doctor Mac'* and in the poem *THE TWA HERDS* - *'McGill has wrought us meikle wae.'* Rev. McGill was friendly with the poet's father and highly regarded by the poet. In a letter dated December, 1789 to Graham of Fintry, Burns described McGill as — 'one of the worthiest, as well as one of the ablest, of the whole priesthood.'

6. Rev. Dr. William Dalrymple — As described earlier.

7. David McWhinnie — An Ayr lawyer who raised 20 subscriptions for the poet's Kilmarnock Edition. Burns wrote to him from Mossgiel in a letter dated 17 April, 1786.

8. John Kennedy — Keeper of the 'drowsy dungeon-clock' of Ayr Tolbooth which was referred to in the poem *THE BRIGS OF AYR.*

Also see: Castlehill; Dungeon-Clock; Whitehill.

AYR GRAMMAR SCHOOL
Map Ref. 335 222

It is known that in 1773 Burns attended the school for 3 weeks but there is conflicting evidence on the location of the school he attended.

A plaque on the east wall of the shop at No. 4 Sandgate, Ayr, purports to indicate the site of the grammar school attended by the poet. The same location is shown for the school in a street plan of Ayr for the period 1534 to 1624.

In Dr. John Strawhorn's History of Ayr Academy (1983), the site of the school attended by Burns is indicated as being in Fort Street, opposite the west end of Academy Street, on the site of the present Academy. This site is supported by Armstrong's 1775 Map of Ayrshire and is accepted as correct.

John Murdoch, who had taught Robert and Gilbert Burnes at Alloway from 1765 to 1768, and then moved to Dumfries, returned to Ayr in 1773 and was appointed English Master at Ayr Grammar School. In the autumn of 1773, Robert attended the school for 3 weeks to improve his English and French and was also encouraged to try Latin.

The poet was accompanied by John Tennant, Jnr., of Laigh Corton Farm, Alloway and later Auchenbay Farm, Ochiltree. While attending the school, the boys shared lodgings in John Murdoch's home in Sandgate. In manhood, John Tennant recalled having been kept awake by the poet reciting verses he had composed.

John Tennant's uncle, David Tennant, youngest brother of John Tennant, Snr., of Laigh Corton and Glenconner Farms, was English Teacher and later Head English Teacher at Ayr Grammar School.

It was David Tennant who recommended John Murdoch, an 18 year old former pupil of Ayr Grammar School, to the poet's father, William Burnes, in 1765, as a teacher for the children of Alloway.

Soon after William Burnes moved to Alloway, he became friendly with Alexander Paterson who had been Latin Master of the Grammar School from 1751 and became Rector in 1761. The friendship probably arose from their both being from the east coast of Scotland. Paterson lent Burnes books to help with his efforts to educate his sons, Robert and Gilbert. After Paterson's death in 1768, his widow continued to lend books to the Burnes family and did much to increase the scope of the poet's literary experience.

Also see: Auchenbay Farm; Ayr; Laigh Corton Farm; Murdoch's House.

AYR RIVER
Map Ref. 323 227

The river rises in the hills north-east of Glenbuck, on the Ayrshire/Lanarkshire border, and flows westwards for about 33 miles to enter the Firth of Clyde in Ayr, at the Map Reference shown.

Burns was familiar with most of the course of the river and it features prominently in Burns lore. Many locations, such as Ballochmyle, Barskimming, Failford, Stair, Leglen Woods and the town of Ayr are well known names in Scottish literature due to their association with the poet.

There are many direct references to the river in the poet's works and in the poem THE BRIGS OF AYR, he described its course from its source to the sea.

Also see: Ayr; Ballochmyle; Barskimming; Bridge Holm; Brigs of Ayr; Ducat Stream; Failford; Glenbuck; Leglen Woods; Ratton-Key; Stair; Stairaird.

BACHELORS' CLUB
Map Ref. 432 272

The premises known as the Bachelors' Club are situated in Sandgate, Tarbolton, a few yards from The Cross. The building was purchased by The National Trust for Scotland in 1951 and is now open to the public as a museum.

When Burns was in Tarbolton Parish, the building was used as an ale house by one John Richard. The stair at the rear of the building, giving access to the

Sandgate, Tarbolton with the Bachelors' Club on the left and Cross Keys Inn on the right.

upper storey, has been reversed from its original position.

Burns, his brother Gilbert, and 5 other young men met in the premises on 11 November, 1780 and founded a debating society called the Bachelors' Club. The poet was elected President for the first meeting.

The 5 young men who joined Robert and Gilbert were, Hugh Reid, Alexander Brown, Thomas Wright, William McGavin and Walter Mitchell. Members admitted later included the poet's friend David Sillar and Matthew Paterson who eventually married Ann Ronald who was referred to by Burns in the poem *THE RONALDS OF THE BENNALS.*

A set of rules for the Club was drawn up at the first meeting and the quality of the wording suggests the mind of the poet. One rule in particular, while identifying the type of person to be admitted to membership, revealed much about the young country lads who were the founders of the Club:- 'Every man proper for a member of this Society, must have a frank, honest, open heart; above anything dirty or mean and must be a professed lover of one or more of the female sex. No haughty, self-conceited person, who looks upon himself as superior to the rest of the Club, and especially no mean-spirited, worldly mortal, whose only will is to heap up money shall upon any pretence whatever be admitted.'

Amongst the subjects listed for debate were:- 'Whether do we derive more happiness from love or friendship?' and 'Whether is the savage man or the peasant of a civilised country in the most happy situation?'

On 4 July, 1781 Burns was initiated into Lodge St. David Tarbolton at a meeting in the Bachelors' Club building.

Also see: Freemasonry; Manson's Inn; Tarbolton.

BACK CAUSEWAY   Map Ref. 498 273

The street in Mauchline now called Castle Street, which runs west from The Cross at the Map Reference shown, was originally called Back Causeway. At the time of Burns, it was the main thoroughfare into Mauchline from the north.

It was in Back Causeway that Burns and Jean Armour set up home in 1788. The house was then owned by Archibald Meikle, known locally as Baldy Muckle, described as 'A tailor in Machlin.' In 1915, the house was bought for the Burns Federation and is now open to the public as a museum.

Back Causeway, Mauchline circa 1920 with Burns's House on the left
and Nance Tannock's Inn on the right.

The neighbouring house was owned by the poet's friend and physician, Doctor John Mackenzie, who may have occupied it as either a house or surgery. It was purchased by the Burns Federation in 1917 and forms part of the museum with the Burns House. Doctor Mackenzie married Helen Miller, daughter of John Miller of the Sun Inn, Mauchline. Helen was Miss Miller of the poem *THE BELLES OF MAUCHLINE*.

Nance Tannock's Inn was also in Back Causeway.

Robin Gibb, Beadle and Bellringer of Mauchline Parish Kirk, lived in a house called 'Brownlea' in Back Causeway. It was situated on the east side of the street, at its junction with the Knowe. Gibb was referred to by Burns as 'Clinkumbell' in the poem *THE HOLY FAIR* — '*Now Clinkumbell, wi rattlin tow, Begins to jow and croon.*' Mary Morrison may also have lived in 'Brownlea'.

Also see: Mary Morison's House; Mauchline, Nance Tannock's Inn; Museums, etc.; Sma' Inn; Sun Inn.

BAILIE GREENSHIELD'S HOUSE   Map Ref. 424 378

This house is no longer extant. It was situated on the north side of Grange Street, Kilmarnock on the site now occupied by the Department of Employment offices at No. 17.

Bailie Thomas Greenshield of Townend had a brewery on the Grange Street site and his house was part of the complex. Burns is reputed to have visited the house and dined with his friend, the Bailie, while visiting Kilmarnock on market days.

Also see: Kilmarnock.

BALLOCHMYLE   Map Ref. 522 264
    The mansion house and estate are situated on the west side on the B705
Mauchline/Catrine Road, one mile south of Mauchline. The house is semi-derelict
and the estate is occupied by Ballochmyle Hospital.

BALLOCHMYLE HOUSE circa 1850

    When Burns moved into Mossgiel Farm, Mauchline, in 1784, Ballochmyle
was owned by Sir John Whitefoord. The men had met as fellow-masons and
continued to do so. Sir John suffered financially by the collapse of the Ayr Bank
in 1772 and was eventually forced to sell Ballochmyle. When the family moved
out, Burns composed the song *FAREWELL TO BALLOCHMYLE*, also called
THE BRAES OF BALLOCHMYLE. In a copy of Johnson's Musical Museum
presented to Captain Riddell of Glenriddell, Burns added the following footnote
to the song — 'I composed the verses on the amiable and excellent family of
Whitefoord leaving Ballochmyle.' The 'Maria' referred to in the song was Sir
John's daughter, Mary Anne Whitefoord.

BALLOCHMYLE FOG HOUSE
Where Burns met 'The Bonie Lass'

The Braes of Ballochmyle is the wooded north bank of the River Ayr between Catrine and the Howford Bridge on the A76 Mauchline/Auchinleck Road.

In 1785, Ballochmyle was bought by Claud Alexander. His sister, Wilhelmina Alexander was the heroine of the song *THE LASS OF BALLOCHMYLE*. Shortly after the Alexanders moved in, Burns was walking by the River Ayr where it flows through the estate when he saw Miss Alexander walking alone. He composed the song soon afterwards and sent a copy of it to her but she failed to even acknowledge receipt. In later life, when Burns was recognised as a poetic genius and Wilhelmina Alexander was an elderly spinster, she was pleased to acknowledge that she had been '*The Bonie Lass*'.

Claud Alexander erected a wooden summer-house, called the Fog House, to commemorate the site where Burns had met Wilhelmina. Unfortunately, it was destroyed by fire by vandals in 1944.

Also see: Catrine; Cloncaird; Mossgiel Farm.

BALLOCHNEIL FARM AND MILL   Map Ref. 223 065

Situated on the east side of the A77 Ayr/Girvan Road, 2 miles south of Kirkoswald. The ruin of the original Ballochneil can be seen behind the existing cottage of that name.

At the time of Burns, the tenant of Ballochneil was Robert Niven, son of John Niven, blacksmith, Ardlochan or Damhouse of Ardlochan, Maidens.

Robert Niven of Ballochneil is thought to have been the prototype of the '*Miller*' in the poem *TAM O'SHANTER*. Douglas Graham, Shanter Farm, Maidens, prototype for Tam in the poem *TAM O'SHANTER*, also farmed Laigh Park, a neighbouring farm to Ballochneil.

Hugh Brown, miller, Damhouse of Ardlochan, Maidens, a neighbour of Douglas Graham's Shanter Farm, is also said to have been the prototype for the '*Miller*' of the poem.

Samuel Broun, the poet's maternal uncle, was son-in-law of Robert Niven and lived at Ballochneil. According to Dr Robert Chambers, the Brouns lived in a room attached to the mill.

OLD BALLOCHNEIL FARM circa 1900

In 1775, Burns attended Hugh Rodger's school in Kirkoswald and while doing so he lodged at Ballochneil. It is disputed whether he lodged with his uncle or with the Niven family. Tradition maintains that he shared a bed with Robert Niven's son, John Niven who was a fellow pupil at Rodger's school and thereafter a life-long friend of the poet.

Also see: Ardlochan; Damhouse of Ardlochan; Kirkoswald; Laigh Park Farm; Maybole; Park Farm; Rodger's House and School.

BARQUHARRIE FARM   Map Ref. 503 191

Situated 1½ miles south of the A70 Ayr/Cumnock Road, a half mile east of Ochiltree. It was the home of George Reid, husband of Agnes Tennant, eldest daughter of John Tennant of Glenconner. John Tennant and his family were all close friends of the poet.

Burns borrowed a horse from George Reid to carry him from Mauchline to Edinburgh and in a letter dated 29 November, 1786 from Edinburgh he apologised to Reid for the delay in returning 'the pownie'.

Also see: Auchenbay Farm; Glenconner Farm; Orangefield.

BARR MILL   Map Ref. 510 368

The mill is no longer extant. It was situated on the south bank of the River Irvine, between the river and what is now Henrietta Street, Galston. The area is still known as Barr Mill.

In a copy of Johnson's Musical Museum presented by Burns to Captain Robert Riddell of Glenriddell, Dumfries, the poet wrote foot-notes to most of the songs. After the old Scottish song I Had A Horse And I Had Nae Mair, he wrote — 'This story is founded on fact. A John Hunter, ancestor to a very respectable farming family, who live in a place in the parish (I think) of Galston, called Barr Mill, was the luckless hero who 'had a horse and had nae mair.' For some little youthful follies he found it necessary to make a retreat to the West Highlands, where he 'feed himself to a Highland laird', for that is the expression of all the oral editions of the song I have heard. The present Mr. Hunter, who told me the anecdote, is the great grandchild of our hero.'

It is thought that Burns met Mr Hunter at a meeting of Loudoun Newmilns Masonic Lodge. It appears from his "Parish (I think) of Galston" that he was not familiar with Barr Mill which is surprising as he was well acquainted with the Galston/Newmilns area.

BARR VILLAGE

Situated on the B734, 6½ miles south-east of Girvan. It is referred to in the poem THE KIRK'S ALARM — 'Barr Steenie! Barr Steenie! What mean ye? What mean ye?' This is a reference to the Rev. Stephen Young, Minister of Barr from 1780 to 1819. The Kirk was on the site of the present kirkyard but can not be traced. The fabric of the original kirk was probably used in the building of the present kirk. Rev. Young is thought to have been buried in the kirkyard but this can not be verified.

An aunt of Burns, described as from Kirkoswald and probably the wife of his maternal uncle, Samuel Broun, is recorded as having said that the poet wrote the song MY NANIE, O' to a girl called Agnes McIlwraith of Pinvalley, whom he had met at Kirkdamdie Fair. At least three other girls are said to have been the heroine of the song.

Kirkdamdie Fair, also called Kirkdominie Fair, was the largest feeing fair in south Ayrshire. It was ancient in origin and was held annually on the last day of May on the grounds of a ruined church on the north bank of the River Stinchar, 1½ miles south-west of Barr.

Also see: Coldcothill Farm; Doura Farm; Kirkoswald; Peggy Thomson's House; Pinvalley; Ship Inn; Stinchar River.

BARSKIMMING   Map Ref. 483 254
The house and estate are situated north of the Mauchline/Stair Road, 1½ miles south-west of Mauchline. The house is still inhabited. When Burns was in Mauchline, Barskimming was the home of Sir Thomas Miller of Glenlee who became Lord Barskimming and later Lord Glenlee. The poet was very familiar with the estate and often walked by the River Ayr which flows through it. Lord Barskimming and the estate are referred to in the 20th stanza of the poem *THE VISION* — *'Thro' many a wild, romantic grove ... An aged judge I saw him rove.'*

Patrick Miller of Daiswinton, Dumfries, patron of Burns and landlord of Ellisland Farm, was Lord Barskimming's brother.

Lord Barskimming's son, Sir William Miller, succeeded to the Barskimming title; he was referred to as *'Barskimming's guid Knight'* in the poem *SECOND ELECTION BALLAD*. He also succeeded to the title Lord Glenlee.
Also see: Barskimming Mill; Bridge Holm.

BARSKIMMING MILL   Map Ref. 492 254
Situated on the River Ayr, south of the Mauchline/Stair Road, 2 miles south-west of Mauchline. The mill building still exists but it stopped milling flour in the 1950's. When Burns was in Mauchline, the miller was the poet's friend, James Andrew. Andrew is buried in Stair kirkyard.

On the north side on the Mauchline/Stair Road, opposite the road leading to the mill, there is a grass area in a bend of the River Ayr, called Bridge Holm. The poet and James Andrew were walking together on the Holm when Burns composed the poem *MAN WAS MADE TO MOURN*.
Also see: Bridge Holm.

BEECHGROVE COTTAGE AND HOUSE   Map Ref. 499 272

The cottage was situated on the west side of Cowgate, at its junction with Catrine Road, Mauchline. The site is now occupied by a property called Grove cottage. It was the home of Peter Morrison, carpenter, cabinet maker, and friend of Burns. He made the furniture for Ellisland Farm, Dumfries and in a letter dated 22 January, 1789, Burns wrote and asked him to speed up his work.

Local tradition maintains that while Burns was at Mossgiel he was in the habit of joining the Morrison family for lunch after Sunday morning church services and that on one such visit he composed the poem *ADDRESS TO THE HAGGIS*. It is thought that only the last stanza was composed initially as a grace before a meal and that the poem was completed later. Other traditions maintain that the poem was written in Edinburgh or at a social evening at Craigie.

Beechgrove House, still occupied and with the same name, is on the south side of the cottage. When Burns was in Mauchline it was owned by his friend, Gavin Hamilton, and was later occupied by Hamilton's son, Doctor Dugald Hamilton.

BEGBIE'S INN
The Inn was in Kilmarnock town centre. The area has been completely re-developed and the site is now under a supermarket in Kilmarnock shopping centre. Begbie's was referred to in the poem *THE ORDINATION* — *'Then aff to Begbie's in a raw, An' drink divine libations.'* In the Rob Rhymer manuscript of the poem, Burns changed the name to 'Crookes', another town centre inn of the period.

Begbie's Inn later became The Angel Hotel and was extant as such for many years.
Also see: Crookes's.

BENNALS FARM   Map Ref. 405 263
    Situated one mile north of the A758 Ayr/Mauchline Road at the east end of
Mossblown. It was the home of William Ronald and his wife and two daughters,
the subjects of the poem *THE RONALDS OF THE BENNALS*. The elder
daughter, Jean Ronald, was courted by the poet's brother Gilbert Burns, but she
married John Reid, Langlands Farm, Tarbolton. The poet was keen to court the
younger daughter, Ann Ronald, but was afraid of being rebuffed because of the
family's wealth and standing. Ann married Matthew Paterson, a Tarbolton
acquaintance of the poet and a member of The Bachelors' Club. William Ronald
eventually went bankrupt and in a letter dated November, 1789 to his brother,
William Burns, the poet referred to Ronald's misfortune — 'Mr. Ronald is
bankrupt, etc.'
Also see: Aikenbrae Farm; Blackbyre; Braehead; Ford; Langlands Farm; Monkton.

BLACKBYRE
    Burns referred to Blackbyre in the poem *THE RONALDS OF THE
BENNALS* — 'The laird o' Blackbyre wad gang through the fire' — but gave no
indication of the location of the property. There is no Blackbyre in the immediate
vicinity of Bennals at present nor was there in Armstrong's 1775 Map of Ayrshire.
Also see: Bennals Farm.

BLACKSIDEND   Map Ref. 585 298
    Blacksidend Hill is located 3 miles north-east of Sorn. It is referred to in the
poem *A MAUCHLINE WEDDING* — 'The rising sun o'er Blacksideen, Was just
appearing fairly*. The 1342 feet high hill lies almost due east from Mossgiel and from
the farm Burns would see the sun rising from behind it.
Also see: Mossgiel Farm.

BOGHEAD FARM   Map Ref. 435 298
    Situated on the south side of the A719 Ayr/Galston Road, 1½ miles east of the
B730 Dundonald/Tarbolton Road. It is a neighbouring farm to Lochlea and was
occupied by James Grieve who was referred to in the poem *EPITAPH ON JAMES
GRIEVE* — 'Here lies Boghead amang the dead, In hopes to get salvation.' In the
dispute between the poet's father, William Burnes, and his landlord, David
McLure, over Lochlea, James Grieve acted as arbitrator on behalf of McLure.
Also see: Lochlea Farm.

BOWLING GREEN HOUSE   Map Ref. 428 382
    An inn, the site of which was on the east side of Portland Street, Kilmarnock,
opposite the north side of West George Street. It was demolished when the former
East George Street was developed. The inn took its name from the nearby
Kilmarnock Bowling Green which, between 1780 and 1790, was located in the
area now occupied by the shop premises at the north-east corner of Portland
Street and West George Street.
    Many of the poet's friends, including Tam Samson, frequented the inn and
bowling green. Tam Samson was referred to in the poems *TAM SAMSON'S
ELEGY* and *TAM SAMSON'S EPITAPH*. Legend maintains that the poems were
composed and recited for the first time in the inn. Tam Samson had been out
shooting and was late in returning. Burns was in the inn and was told by Tam's
nephew, Charles Samson, that Tam had said that he would be happy to die out
shooting on the moors. Burns retired for a short time and by the time Tam
returned, the poet was able to read the poem *TAM SAMSON'S ELEGY*. After
protests from Tam, the poet composed and recited *TAM SAMSON'S EPITAPH*
and its 'Per Contra' to let the world know that Tam was hale and hearty.
    The innkeeper was Sandy Patrick, Tam Samson's son-in-law.
Also see: Kilmarnock; Laigh Kirk; Ochiltree; Tam Samson's House.

BRAEHEAD

The location is referred to in the poem *THE RONALDS OF THE BENNALS* — '*The laird o' Braehead has been on his speed, For mair than a tow-mond or twa, man.*' The poet gave no indication of the property to which he was referring and the subject has caused much speculation. There is no property called Braehead in the immediate vicinity of Bennals but there are several in neighbouring parishes.

MARGARET
CHALMERS

BRAEHEAD FARM   Map Ref. 496 248

Situated on Haugh Road, Mauchline, 2 miles south of the town. Margaret 'Peggy' Chalmers, friend of Burns, lived at the farm, probably while the poet was at Mossgiel but it is not known whether or not they met at that time. The dates between which the family lived at Braehead are not known. She was born at Fingland, Kirkcudbrightshire and moved to Mauchline when financial difficulties forced her father to sell his estate.

Burns visited Peggy Chalmers at Harvieston, near Dollar in October, 1787 during his Highland tour. She claimed later that he had eventually proposed marriage to her and the tone of his letters to her suggests that he probably did so. Peggy was referred to in the love songs, *MY PEGGY'S FACE* and *WHERE BRAVING ANGRY WINTER'S STORM.*

BRAEHEAD HOUSE, KILMARNOCK   Map Ref. 434 381

The house was situated to the north of London Road, Kilmarnock on the eminence overlooking Kilmarnock Water. It was demolished several years ago. The present Braehead Court and Kilmarnock Technical College occupy the site. Braehead was the home of William Paterson, Town Clerk of Kilmarnock and friend of Burns. The neighbouring property on the south side of London Road was Rosebank, home of Thomas Samson, subject of the poems *TAM SAMSON'S ELEGY* and *TAM SAMSON'S EPITAPH.* Tam Samson's nephew, Charles Samson, was clerk to William Paterson.

Braehead House, Kilmarnock is unlikely to have been the 'Braehead' referred to in the poem *THE RONALDS OF THE BENNALS* as the poem was composed before the poet frequented Kilmarnock.

At the time of Burns, the house sat on a hill on the outskirts of the town, overlooking the town centre, Kilmarnock Water and the Laigh and High Kirks.
Also see: Kilmarnock; Tam Samson's House.

BRAEHEAD HOUSE

BRIDGE HOLM   Map Ref. 491 254
     Situated on the south bank of the River Ayr, immediately west of
Barskimming Bridge on the Mauchline/Stair Road, 2 miles south-west of
Mauchline. It is also known as Miller's Holm. Burns composed the dirge *MAN
WAS MADE TO MOURN* while walking on the Holm.
     Tradition maintains that the poet was interested in a girl called Kate Kemp
who lived with her father in a house on the west side of the Mauchline/Stair Road
at the north end of Barskimming Bridge. One evening he walked from Mossgiel to
Barskimming, hoping to meet Kate. Near the bridge he met his friend, James
Andrew, the Miller of Barskimming Mill, who was also interested in Kate.

BARSKIMMING BRIDGE and KATE KEMP'S HOUSE

Together they met Kate's father who told them that she had gone out to look for their cow that had strayed. Burns and Andrew went walking on the grassy holm by the river. After some time the poet appeared to be pre-occupied and eventually left Andrew to return to Mossgiel. When next they met Burns apologised to the miller and explained that he had been composing . poem. He then recited *MAN WAS MADE TO MOURN.*
Also see: Barskimming; Barskimming Mill; Haugh.

BRIDGE HOUSE   Map Ref. 330 195
    The house is no longer extant. It was situated on the east side of the A719 Ayr/Doonfoot Road, near the main entrance to Belleisle Park. About 1843, the poet's youngest sister, Isabella Burns Begg, who had been married and living in East Lothian, moved into Bridge House. She lived there until her death in 1858,

ISABELLA
BURNS BEGG

aged 87 years, and was buried in Alloway Kirkyard beside her father, William Burnes. She was survived by her unmarried daughters, Agnes and Isabella Begg who lived on in Bridge House. Agnes died in 1883 and Isabella in 1886. The death of Isabella Begg marked the end of the last direct family link with the poet in Alloway.
    During Isabella Burns Begg's years in Bridge House, her home was a place of pilgrimage for Burns enthusiasts. She gave a vast amount of information about her famous brother, Robert Burns, but as she was 12 years younger than the poet her accounts of his life, especially until he reached manhood, cannot be relied upon for accuracy. Isabella always spoke highly of her brother, especially of his interest in and the attention to the younger members of the family. She was interviewed by Dr. Robert Chambers, author of a Life of Burns (1851/52), and recounted for him a story composed by Burns as a teenager for his wee brothers and sisters at Lochlea. Chambers published the story in his book Nursery Rhymes Of Scotland with Burns shown as the author. It is written as it would be narrated by the poet in the Ayrshire dialect of the time, and is called —

                The Marriage Of Robin Redbreast and Jenny Wren.
    "There was an auld grey poussie baudrons (cat), and she gaed awa' doon by a water side, and there she saw a wee Robin Redbreast happin' (hopping) on a brier (briar); and poussie baudrons says, 'Whare's tu gaun, wee Robin?' And wee Robin says, "I'm gaun awa' to the King to sing him a sang this guid Yule

mornin'." And poussie baudrons says, "Come here, wee Robin, and I'll let ye see a bonnie white ring roun' my neck." But wee Robin says, "Na, Na! gray poussie baudrons; na, na! Ye worry't (molested) the wee mousie, but ye'se no worry me." So wee Robin flew awa' till he cam' to a fail fauld-dike (turf foldwall), and there he saw a grey greedy gled (hawk) sittin'. And the grey greedy gled says, "Whare's tu gaen, wee Robin?" And wee Robin says, "I'm gaun awa' to the King to sing him a sang this guid Yule mornin'." And grey greedy gled says, "Come here, wee Robin, and I'll let ye see a bonnie feather in my wing. But wee Robin says, Na, Na! grey greedy gled; na, na! Ye pookit (plucked) a' the wee lintie (linnet), but ye'se no pook me." So wee Robin flew awa' till he cam' to the cleuch (cleft) o' a craig (crag), and there he saw slee (sly) Tod Lowrie (fox) sittin'. And Slee Tod Lowrie says, "Whare's tu gaen, wee Robin?" And wee Robin says, "I'm gaun awa' to the King to sing him a sang this guid Yule mornin'." And slee Tod Lowrie says, "Come here, wee Robin, and I'll let ye see a bonnie spot on the tap o' my tail." But wee Robin says, "Na, na! slee Tod Lowrie; na, na! Ye worry't (molested) the wee lammie (lamb), but ye'se no worry me." So wee Robin flew awa' till he cam' to a bonnie burnside, and there he saw a wee callant (boy) sittin'. And the wee callant says, "Whare's tu gaen, wee Robin?" And wee Robin says, "I'm gaun awa' to the King to sing him a sang this guid Yule mornin'." and the wee callant says, "Come here wee Robin, and I'll gie ye a wheen grand moolins (crumbs) oot o' my pooch (pocket)." But wee Robin says, "Na, na! wee callant; na, na! Ye speldert (tore apart) the gowdspink (goldfinch), but ye'se no spelder me." So wee Robin flew awa' till he cam' to the King, and there he sat on a winnock-sole (window-ledge) and sang the King a bonnie sang. And the King says to the Queen, "What'll we gie to wee Robin for singin' us this bonnie sang?" And the Queen says to the King, " I think we'll gie him the wee Wren to be his wife." So wee Robin and the wee Wren were married, and the King and the Queen and a' the coort danced at the waddin'; syne (soon) he flew awa' hame to his ain water side and happit (hopped) on a brier."

'I'll be a brig when ye're a shapeless cairn'
(The 'New' bridge being dismantled after its collapse in 1877).

BRIGS OF AYR   Map Ref. 336 223 and 338 222
    The two bridges span the River Ayr in Ayr town centre. They are referred
to in the poem *THE BRIGS OF AYR*. The Auld Brig, probably built about 1232,
is still in use as a busy footbridge. Until 1786 it was the only bridge over the river
in or near the town. It was extensively restored in 1910. The history of the bridge
and the story of its restoration can be read in the book Brig Of Ayr by James A
Morris (1910).
    The New Brig of the poem was on the site of the bridge furthest
downstream at present. The new bridge referred to in the poem, having been built
in 1786, collapsed in a flood in 1877, as prophesied by the Auld Brig in the
poem —'I'll be a brig when ye're a shapeless cairn.'
Also see: Ducat Stream.

BURNS COTTAGE   Map Ref. 335 186
    Situated on the west side on the B7024 Ayr/Maybole Road, in Alloway
Village, 2 miles south of Ayr town centre. In 1756, the poet's father William
Burnes, feued 7½ acres of land from Doctor Alexander Campbell, Ayr. He built a
cottage on the land and called the property New Gardens, intending to work the
ground as a market garden.
    Robert Burns was born in the cottage on 25 January, 1759. When he was 9
or 10 days old, the south gable of the house was blown down in a storm and —
'Twas then a blast o' Janwar win', Blew hansel in on Robin' — as the poet
recorded in his song *THERE WAS A LAD*.
    When the poet was one day old he was baptised in the cottage by the Rev.
William Dalrymple of Ayr Auld Kirk. The witnesses were John Tennant and James
Young. Nothing is known of James Young. It is generally accepted that John
Tennant was the farmer at Laigh Corton and later Glenconner, a friend of both
the poet and his father. It is much more likely that the witness was John Tennant,
blacksmith, Alloway, whose smiddy (smithy) was close to Burns cottage. The site
of the smiddy, still called Smithy Cottage, is at No. 6 Main Street, Alloway. The
blacksmith's wife is thought to have been a midwife at the poet's birth and also
the *'gossip'* who *'keekit in his loof'*, according to the song *THERE WAS A LAD*.

BURNS COTTAGE

A woman called Betty Davidson, an elderly relation of the poet's mother, lodged with the family in the cottage. Burns later recalled that she had a fund of stories about the supernatural and the young Burns probably had his imagination fired by her tales.

In 1766, when Burns was 7 years of age, the family moved from the cottage to Mount Oliphant Farm, about 2 miles away. William Burnes retained the cottage and rented it out until 1781. The Ayrshire Register of Sasines shows that on 4 August, 1781 the property was transferred from William Burnes, Farmer, Lochlea (to which they had moved from Mount Oliphant) to the Incorporation of Shoemakers, Ayr.

From 1781 to 1881, the shoemakers rented it out as an ale house and it fell into a state of some disrepair. It was not totally neglected as in 1847 the building which now houses the museum was built as a meeting hall. In 1881 the property was purchased by the Burns Monument Trustees. The Trustees restored the cottage and it was opened to the public in March, 1901 in the form in which we now know it.

It is interesting to note that the first recorded dinner to pay tribute to the memory of Robert Burns — the first Burns Supper — was held in the cottage. During the summer of 1801 a group of the poet's friends and admirers sat down to dinner, including sheep's head and haggis. The poem *ADDRESS TO A HAGGIS* was read and several toasts were drunk. A portrait of the poet painted on wood and intended as a sign for the cottage was presented to the company and an Ode On The Anniversary of Burns was read by its author, The Rev. Hamilton Paul, a noted Burns scholar. Nine gentlemen were present:-

William Crawford, Doonside, Ayr.
John Ballantine, lawyer, Castlehill, Ayr, to whom the poem *THE BRIGS OF AYR* was dedicated.
Robert Aiken, lawyer, Whitehill, Ayr, to whom the poem *THE COTTER'S SATURDAY NIGHT* was dedicated.
Dr Patrick Douglas, Garallan, Cumnock, the poet's patron who arranged a post for him in Jamaica.
Primrose Kennedy, Drummelland, Maybole.
Hugh Ferguson, barrackmaster, Ayr.
David Scott, banker, Ayr.
Thomas Jackson, rector of Ayr Academy.
The Rev. Hamilton Paul, Burns scholar, elected Chaplain and Laureate.

The gathering resolved to meet again in the cottage on 29 January, 1802. It was thought then that the poet's birthday was 29 January. They duly met as arranged, joined by Provost William Bowie of Ayr and other 8 leading citizens.

An excellent Burns museum is in the grounds of the cottage.

Also see: Alloway; Castlehill House; Doonside House; Garallan House; Museums, etc; New Gardens; Whitehill.

CAPRINGTON   Map Ref. 405 363
The castle and estate are situated 2 miles south-west of Kilmarnock, between the A759 Kilmarnock/Troon Road and the B7038 Kilmarnock/Ayr Road. In a note to a suppressed stanza of the poem *THE VISION*, the poet indicated that the following lines refer to Caprington — '*And Irwine, marking out the bound, Enamour'd of the scenes around, Slow runs his race, A name I doubly honor'd found, With knightly grace.*' The poet must have been familiar with the estate. In 1786, when Jean Armour's father took out a warrant against him, Burns went into hiding with his uncle and aunt at Fairlie Estate within a short distance of Caprington. As an admirer of the Scottish patriot, William Wallace, he would have known of the legends connecting Wallace with Caprington.

Also see: Fairlie House; Old Rome.

CARNELL HOUSE   Map Ref. 467 323
Situated east of the A719 Ayr/Galston Road, one mile south-west of its junction with the A76 Kilmarnock/Mauchline Road, and on the west bank of the River Cessnock. The house is still occupied. It is about 2 miles from Lochlea Farm and was called Cairnhill when Burns lived in the area.

In 1781, when the poet was 22 years of age, he courted a girl called Alison (Ellison) Begbie who worked at Carnell. She lived at Old Place Farm on the east bank of the Cessnock, about one mile downstream from Carnell. The poet wrote five romantic letters to Alison and she is thought to have been the heroine of the songs *THE LASS OF CESSNOCK BANK* and *BONNIE PEGGY ALISON* (And I'll Kiss Thee Yet). He proposed marriage to her but was rejected.

In a dispute between the poet's father, William Burnes, and his landlord, David McLure, over the terms of the lease of Lochlea Farm, Burnes claimed an allowance for the purchase of 12 tons of limestone annually from Cairnhill Lime Quarry, to fertilise the fields of the farm.

Cairnhill Lime Kilns, which the poet must have visited regularly, were situated about 300 yards north of the A719 Ayr/Galston Road and 400 yards east of the Fiveways/Riccarton Road.
Also see: Mary Morison's House; Old Place; Old Rome.

CARRICK
An ancient division of Ayrshire, being that part of the county south of the River Doon. The other divisions are Cunninghame and Kyle. The poet made several references to Carrick, the best known being in the song *MY FATHER WAS A FARMER* — '*My father was a farmer upon the Carrick border.*'

An entry by the poet in his First Commonplace Book, dated August, 1784, referred to Kyle, Carrick and Cunninghame — 'My dear native country, the ancient Baileries of Carrick, Kyle and Cunningham.... We have never had one Scotch poet of any eminence, to make the fertile banks of Irvine, the romantic woodlands and sequestered scenes of Ayr, and the healthy, mountainous source and winding sweep of Doon, emulate Tay, Forth, Ettrick and Tweed.'
Also see: Cunninghame; Kyle.

CASSILIS DOWNANS   Map Ref. 341 128
Green hillocky land west of the B7045 Dalrymple/Maybole Road, about 2 miles south of Dalrymple. Cassilis is pronounced 'Castles'. It was referred to in the opening stanza of the poem *HALLOWE'EN* — '*Upon that night, when fairies light, On Cassilis Downans dance.*' The area takes its name from Cassilis House which is located at the Map Reference shown.

JOHN BALLANTINE

CASTLEHILL HOUSE   Map Ref. 354 202
The house was situated east of the A713 Ayr/Dalmellington Road, 1½ miles south of Ayr town centre. The house is no longer extant but gave its name to the Castlehill district of Ayr. It was the home of John Ballantine, lawyer and banker who became Provost of Ayr in 1787. Ballantine was a friend and patron of Burns and corresponded with him over several years. The poem *THE BRIGS OF AYR* was inscribed to Ballantine.
Also see: Ayr Auld Kirk; Burns Cottage.

CATRINE
Situated on the B705 Mauchline/Auchinleck Road, 2½ miles south of Mauchline, and on the banks of the River Ayr. It was referred to in the poem *FAREWELL TO BALLOCHMYLE* or *THE BRAES OF BALLOCHMYLE* — 'The Catrine woods were yellow seen, The flowers decayed on Catrine Lee.' It was also referred to in the poem *THE BRIGS OF AYR* — 'Learning and Worth in equal measure strode, From simple Catrine, their long-loved abode.' 'Learning and Worth' is a reference to Professor Dugald Stewart of Catrine House. In 1786, Professor Stewart introduced Burns to Lord Daer in Catrine House. The meeting is commemorated in the poem *ON MEETING LORD DAER.*
In 1788, Claud Alexander of Ballochmyle, in partnership with the industrial reformer, David Dale, established a cotton mill in the valley of the River Ayr at Catrine and the village was developed to house mill workers. Due to its beautiful location and design, Catrine was a model village for the first 150 years of its existence. Burns must have witnessed the developement of the village.
Also see: Ballochmyle; Catrine House.

CATRINE HOUSE

CATRINE HOUSE   Map Ref. 532 257
Situated on the west side of Townhead, Catrine at its junction with Newton Street. The house was built in 1682 and is still occupied. It was the country home of Dugald Stewart, Professor of Moral Philosophy in Edinburgh University and

patron and friend of Burns. On 23 October, 1786, together with Doctor Mackenzie of Mauchline, Burns was invited to lunch at Catrine House where Professor Stewart introduced him to Lord Daer, second son of the Earl of Selkirk. The meeting was commemorated by the poet in the poem *ON MEETING LORD DAER* — '*A ne'er to be forgotten day, Sae far I sprackl'd up the brae, I dinner'd wi' a Lord!*'

As the house stands on the floor of a steep-sided valley, the poet's expression 'sprackl'd up the brae' has caused.confusion in interpretation. He could have been referring to going up the Howford Brae south of the River Ayr on his likely route to Catrine House (Catrine Village did not exist and it is unlikely that a road existed on the line of the B705 Mauchline/Catrine Road) or referring to his homeward journey. It has been suggested that the poet was referring to his 'ascent of the social ladder' but the use of the word 'sprackl'd' (clambering with difficulty) in this context is hardly in keeping with the character of the poet.

Burns and Professor Stewart were both freemasons. At a meeting of Lodge St. James Tarbolton held in Mauchline on 25 July, 1787, over which the poet presided in his role of Depute Master, Professor Stewart was made an Honorary Member of the Lodge. When the poet was in Edinburgh, the Professor was kind to him and helped to introduce him to prominent members of society.

Also see: Catrine.

CESSNOCK RIVER   Map Ref. 472 375
The Cessnock joins the River Irvine from the south, between Hurlford and Galston, at the Map Reference shown. It was referred to in the song *THE LASS OF CESSNOCK BANK*, which was probably inspired by the poet's early love, Alison (Ellison) Begbie. She lived at Old Place Farm, Crossroads, on the east bank of the Cessnock and worked at Carnell House on the west bank of the river, one mile upstream from her home. The river was also referred to in a suppressed stanza of the poem *THE VISION* — '*Where Cessnock flows with gurgling sound.*'

On a summer evening, walk by the winding, gurgling Cessnock near Carnell and it is easy to imagine the poet and his lass strolling together, unaware that two centuries later they would still be remembered.

The poet's friend, John Goldie of Kilmarnock — '*O Gowdie, terror o' the Whigs*' — subject of the poem *EPISTLE TO JOHN GOLDIE*, was born at Craig Mill on the Cessnock.

Also see: Auchinskeith; Carnell House; Craig Mill; Old Place.

CLONCAIRD   Map Ref. 357 076
Situated on the Water Of Girvan, west of the B7045 Kirkmichael/Straiton Road, one mile south of Kirkmichael. It was the home of James Whitefoord, relative of the poet's patron and friend, Sir John Whitefoord of Ballochmyle. Cloncaird was referred to as '*Glencaird*' in the poem *THE FETE CHAMPETRE* — '*Their vote shall be Glencaird's man.*'

It is not known whether the reference was to Sir John or James Whitefoord but was probably the latter. Sir John had moved to Edinburgh when he sold Ballochmyle in 1785 and the poem was not written until 1788.

COILSFIELD HOUSE   Map Ref. 447 265
The house is no longer extant. It was situated north of the A758 Ayr/Mauchline Road, one mile east of the B730 Tarbolton/Stair Road. It was the home of Colonel Hugh Montgomerie, later 12th Earl of Eglinton, who was referred to as '*Sodger Hugh*' in the poem *THE AUTHOR'S EARNEST CRY AND PRAYER*.

Highland Mary Campbell is thought to have worked at Coilsfield as a dairy maid. In the poem *HIGHLAND MARY*, the poet referred to the house as '*The Castle o' Montgomerie*' and indicated that it was on the 'banks and braes and streams around' that he parted from Mary.

A large thorn tree which stood on the west bank of the Fail Water, about 200 yards north of the mansion house, was known as Mary's Thorn and was reputed to be a trysting place for Burns and Mary Campbell. When the tree collapsed it was cut up and distributed throughout the world.

Coilsfield was demolished and replaced by a new mansion which was called Montgomery House. The House is no longer extant, having been destroyed by fire. 'Montgomerie's Peggy', heroine of the song of that name and one of the most mysterious figures in the works of Burns, worked at Coilsfield while the poet was as Lochlea. Gilbert Burns said that the poet was in the habit of meeting Peggy at Tarboth Mill (Tarbolton or Willie's Mill). Burns wrote — "though I began the affair merely in a 'gaiete de coeur',or, to tell the truth... a vanity of showing my parts in courtship, particularly my abilties at a 'billet-doux'.... When I had battered myself into a very warm affection for her, she told me one day in a flag of truce, that her fortress had been for some time before the rightful property of another." Peggy was engaged to be married to another and Burns ended this courtship.

In a dispute between the poet's father, William Burnes, and his Lochlea landlord, the arbiter on behalf of Burnes was one, Charles Norval of Coilsfield. All that is known about Norval is that he was a gardener at Coilsfield. Tradition maintains that the man referred to as 'whipper-in' in the poem THE TWA DOGS — 'Our whipper-in, wee blastit wonner' — was Hugh Andrew, Huntsman at Coilsfield.

Also see: Fail; Failford; Mauchline Burn; Stairaird; Tarbolton Mill.

COLDCOTHILL FARM   Map Ref. 454 308

Situated a half mile south of the A719 Ayr/Galston Road, 2½ miles east of the B730 Dundonald/Tarbolton Road. It is a neighbouring farm to Lochlea and was said by the poet's brother, Gilbert Burns, to have been the home of Agnes Fleming whom Gilbert said was the heroine of the song MY NANIE O'.

Doura Farm, which also neighbours Lochlea, has also been referred to as the home of Agnes Fleming.

The Ayrshire Register of Sasines shows that when the Burnes family lived in Lochlea, a family called Steven lived in Coldcothill. The Register also shows that one John Fleming was tenent of Doura. It is thought that Agnes Fleming's home was at Doura and that she worked at Coldcothill.

A massive plane tree, said to have been a trysting place for Burns and Agnes Fleming, stood on the hill above Coldcothill until 1949.

The poet's youngest sister, Isabella Burns Begg,said that the heroine of the song MY NANIE, O' was Peggy Thomson of Kirkoswald; the poet's aunt, Mrs Brown of Kirkoswald, said that it was Agnes McIlwraith of Pinvalley, Barr; local tradition in Girvan maintains that it was Nannie Brown, daughter of the proprietor of the Ship Inn, Girvan; and Rev. Hamilton Paul, a 19th century Burns scholar, said that it was an Agnes Sheriff of Kilmarnock. The poet did not identify the heroine.

Also see: Doura Farm; Girvan River; Kirkoswald; Lugar River; Minnybae Farm; Pinvalley, Peggy Thomson's House; Ship Inn; Stinchar River.

COMMONSIDE   Map Ref. 415 244

Situated on the B744 Annbank/Tarbolton Road, one mile east of Annbank. The poet's friend and fellow-rhymer, David Sillar, set up an adventure school at Commonside after he had failed to obtain a post as permanent teacher at Tarbolton school. The post as teacher was given to John Wilson, immortalised by Burns as 'Doctor Hornbook' in the poem DEATH AND DOCTOR HORNBOOK. The Commonside school failed after a short time and David Sillar moved to Irvine. Later in life he inherited wealth and became a respected businessman and member of Irvine Town Council.

Also see: Irvine; Spittalside.

CORSINCON Map Ref. 671 147

A conical shaped hill, 1547 feet high, situated east of the A76 New Cumnock/ Sanquhar Road, 3 miles south of New Cumnock. It is referred to in one of the poet's most beautiful songs which gets less appreciation than it deserves, *O'WERE I ON PARNASSUS HILL — 'On Corsincon I'll glow'r and spell, And write how much I love thee.'* When the song was composed, Burns and Jean Armour were recently married but separated. He was living alone at Isle, Dumfries, preparing Ellisland Farm for her arrival from Mauchline. From the words we can picture Burns in the solitude looking lovingly and longingly north-wards to Corsincon and beyond towards Mauchline and thinking of his young wife. The hill is also referred to in the poem *DOES HAUGHTY GAUL INVASION THREAT — 'The Nith shall run to Corsincon.'*

COWGATE Map Ref. 498 273

Cowgate is a street in Mauchline town centre. It extends south from Loudoun Street, 50 yards west of The Cross. When Burns was in Mauchline area, it was the main route into the village from the south.

COWGATE circa 1875

It was referred to in the poem *THE HOLY FAIR — 'While "common-sense" has taen the road, An' aff an' up the Cowgate.'* Tradition maintains that "common-sense" was a reference to the poet's physician and friend, Doctor John Mackenzie. Shortly before the poem was composed, the doctor had written an article, either on the subject of common-sense or signed 'common-sense' as a nom-de-plume, and possibly in reply to something said or written by Burns. On the day of Mauchline Holy Fair he had arranged to dine with the Earl of Dumfries at Dumfries House, Cumnock and the poet saw him heading out of the village by the Cowgate, just as the Rev. Dr. William Peebles of Newton-on-Ayr was mounting the rostrum to give his oration.

Jean Armour's parental home was in Cowgate, as was Beechgrove Cottage where the poem *ADDRESS TO A HAGGIS* is said to have been composed. The poet's favourite tavern, The Whitefoord Arms, was on the west side on the junction of Cowgate and Loudoun Street and Poosie Nancie's Inn, the setting of the cantata Love and Liberty (The Jolly Beggars) is on the east side on the junction.

Also see: Armour's House; Beechgrove Cottage; Mauchline; Poosie Nancie's Inn; Whitefoord Arms.

COYLE WATER   Map Ref. 396 215

Joins the River Ayr from the south at the Map Reference shown, a half mile upstream from the bridge carrying the B744 Annbank/Belston Road. It is referred to in the poems *THE BRIGS OF AYR* — '*When from the woods where springs the brawling Coil*'. It is also referred to in the song *THE SOLDIER'S RETURN* — '*I thought upon the banks o' Coil*'. Tradition maintains that Millmannoch on the river is the location described in the song as the meeting place of the soldier and his sweetheart.

The name is derived from Coilus, King of the Picts (said to be the original of Old King Cole of the nursery rhyme.) The name Kyle for an ancient division of Ayrshire is also derived from Coilus/Coil. In the poem *THE VISION*, Burns referred to his poetic Muse as Coila.

Also see: Coylton; Kyle.

COYLTON

The modern village is situated on the A70 Ayr/Cumnock Road, 5 miles east of Ayr. The hamlet now called Low Coylton, one mile to the south on the Coylton/Drongan Road, was the original village. The ruined remains of the original parish church are at Low Coylton.

The ruined Kirk at Low Coylton —
including the graves of Rev. Shaw and Nellie Kilpatrick's parents.

The Rev. David Shaw, referred to by Burns in the poem *THE TWA HERDS* as one of '*baith the Shaws*', was Minister at Coylton from 1749 to 1810. He was Moderator of the General Assembly of the Church of Scotland in 1776. Although he lived until he was 91 years of age he was reputed never to have required spectacles for reading or writing. He is buried in the kirkyard at Low Coylton.

Alan Kilpatrick and his wife, Margaret Good, parents of Nellie Kilpatrick, the girl to whom Burns addressed his first song, *HANDSOME NELL*, are also buried in Low Coylton kirkyard. Alan Kilpatrick was miller at Purclewan Mill near Mount Oliphant when the Burnes family lived at the farm; he was born at Millmannoch, between Low Coylton and Drongan.

Tradition maintains that Millmannoch is the location described in the song *THE SOLDIER'S RETURN*. The song relates how the returning soldier — 'thought upon the banks o' Coil' — then — 'reach'd the bonie glen' — and — 'pass'd the mill and trysting thorn'. Millmannoch is recognisable from the description and to describe it as he did, the poet must have been familiar with the area.

On the east side of the Low Coylton/Drongan Road, a half mile south of Low Coylton and 200 yards north of Millmannoch (map ref. 431 185), a thorn bush surrounded by a metal fence is said to be the 'trysting thorn' of the song *THE SOLDIER'S RETURN*.
Also see: Purclewan.

CRAIGENGILLAN HOUSE   Map Ref. 474 028

The house is still occupied. It is situated one mile north of Loch Doon, Dalmellington. It was the home of John McAdam, who was addressed in the poem *TO MR McADAM OF CRAIGEN-GILLAN* — *'I'll cock my nose aboon them a', I'm roos'd by Craigen-Gillan.'* McAdam had written to Burns who responded with the poem, written extempore in Nance Tannock's Inn, Mauchline. In the poem, John McAdam's son, Quinton McAdam, was referred to as *'young Dunaskin's laird.'* Quinton was also referred to in the poem *SECOND HERON ELECTION BALLAD* as *'o' lads no the warst.'*

In a letter from Edinburgh to Doctor Mackenzie, Mauchline, dated 11 January, 1787 Burns made reference to one of John McAdam's daughters as 'the beauty-famed and wealth-celebrated Miss McAdam, our Country-woman.'
Also see: Dunaskin.

CRAIGENTON FARM   Map Ref. 231 055

Situated 2 miles east of Turnberry and to the east of the 'C' class road from Kirkoswald to Girvan. The poet's maternal grandparents and great grandparents farmed at Craigenton. His mother, Agnes Broun, daughter of Gilbert Broun and Agnes Rennie was probably born at Whitestone Cottage, Culzean and moved to Craigenton as an infant when her father joined her grandfather in the farm. She was the eldest of 6 children and her mother died when she was 10 years old. After looking after her brothers and sisters for two years, with the help of Ann Gillespie who later married John Davidson, prototype of Souter Johnie, Agnes went to live

CRAIGENTON FARM

with her maternal grandmother, Mrs Rennie, in Maybole.

Gilbert Broun married 3 times and it is thought that Agnes became estranged from her father and step-mothers, resulting in the poet having little or no contact with his grandfather.

The poet's maternal grandparents and great grandparents are buried in Kirkoswald Kirkyard.

Also see: Kirkoswald; Maybole; Whitestone Cottage.

CRAIGIE VILLAGE   Map Ref. 428 324

Situated between the A77 Ayr/Kilmarnock Road and A719 Ayr/Galston Road. 1½ miles east of the B730 Dundonald/Tarbolton Road.

The poet's friend, the Rev. George Bannatyne, was minister of Craigie Parish Church from 1744 to 1764. After leaving Craigie, he was minister of St. George's Church, Glasgow. As Bannatyne left Craigie 13 years before Burns moved to the nearby farm of Lochlea, it is not known when or how they became acquainted.

The Rev. Andrew Shaw, referred to in the poem THE TWA HERDS as one of 'baith the Shaws', was minister at Craigie from 1765 to 1810. He is buried in Craigie Kirkyard. John Wilson, 'Doctor Hornbook' of the poem DEATH AND DOCTOR HORNBOOK, was school master at Craigie before he moved to Tarbolton in 1781.

The village should not be confused with Craigie House, Ayr, parental home of the poet's friend and patron, Mrs Dunlop of Dunlop. Craigie House took its name from the Wallace family's ancient seat, Craigie Castle near Craigie Village.

Sir John Wallace, Laird of Craigie and ancestor of Mrs Dunlop is referred to in the poem THE VISION as — 'The chief on Sark, who glorious fell in high command.' In 1448, Sir John was wounded in a battle on the banks of the River Sark on the Scottish/English border and died 3 months later at Craigie Castle.

CRAIG MILL   Map Ref. 482 329

Situated on the north bank of the River Cessnock, a few hundred yards east of the A76 Kilmarnock/Mauchline Road. The mill is no longer extant and only the track leading to it and the remnants of the man-made wall of the lade can be traced. It was the parental home of John Goldie or Gowdie, friend of Burns and referred to in the poem EPISTLE TO JOHN GOLDIE — 'O' Gowdie terror o' the Whigs.' Goldie was born at Craig Mill in 1717. He moved to Kilmarnock and started in business as a cabinet maker and later became a prosperous wine merchant with a shop at Kilmarnock Cross. He earned some fame as a writer of religious essays and as a theorist on religious beliefs.

Tradition maintains that Goldie visited Burns at Mossgiel during harvest time in 1785. Burns was working in a field and when Goldie arrived the poet sat down with him behind a stook and recited a few of his compositions. Goldie suggested that Burns should visit him at his home in Kilmarnock; he did so and was introduced to the leading citizens of Kilmarnock, many of whom remained his friends. John Goldie stood surety to John Wilson, printer, for the printing of the Kilmarnock Edition of the poet's work.

CROOKES'S

In the 'Rob Rhymer' manuscript of the poem THE ORDINATION, Burns changed the name 'Begbie's' to 'Crookes's' in the lines originally composed as 'Then aff to Begbie's in a raw, An' drink divine libations.' The line is normally published as 'Begbie's'. The place referred to as 'Crookes's' is unknown. It is generally said to have been an inn in Kilmarnock town centre. Another feasible theory is that it referred to the home of a family called Crookes who were prominent in the leather trade in the town in the 18th century. In support of this theory, the third line of the poem is quoted — 'An' ye wha leather rax an' draw' — but it must be regarded as of little evidential value.

Also see: Begbie's Inn.

Cunningham Street, Tarbolton, circa 1900 with the Cross Keys Inn on the left and Doctor Hornbook's House third from the right.

CROSS KEYS INN   Map Ref. 431 272
The building is no longer extant. It was situated on the south side of Cunningham Street, Tarbolton, on the site now occupied by a public garden. At a meeting in the inn on 8 July, 1782, Lodge St. James Tarbolton was reconstituted. For several years thereafter, the Lodge met in the Inn and Burns was an enthusiastic and regular attender. As Depute Master of the Lodge from 1784 to 1788, he occasionally presided over the meetings.

On 9 August, 1844, the poet's three surviving sons were made Honorary Members of Lodge St. James at a meeting in Cross Keys Inn.

Also see: Freemasonry; Manson's Inn; Museums, etc., Tarbolton.

ROBERT BURNS, Jnr. The poet's eldest son.

COL. W. NICHOL BURNS
The poet's third son.

LIEUT. COL. JAMES GLENCAIRN BURNS
The poet's fourth son.

CROSSRAGUEL   Map Ref. 275 084

Jean Kennedy, the model for *'Kirkton Jean'* of the poem *TAM O'SHANTER*, was the daughter of Alexander Kennedy, Farmer, Crossraguel. No Crossraguel Farm exists at present and it is concluded that Alexander Kennedy had a small farm or was a farm worker in the vicinity of Crossraguel Abbey.

The 13th century abbey is situated on the east side of the A77 Maybole/Girvan Road, one mile south of Maybole. It was a ruin when Burns was a boy in the area. He made no reference to it in his works.

Jean Kennedy, and her sister Anne, kept an inn in Kirkoswald known locally at The Ladies' or Leddies' House. In the poem *TAM O'SHANTER*, Burns referred to it as *'The Lord's House.'*

Also see: Kirkoswald; The Ladies'House.

CULZEAN CASTLE   Map Ref. 232 013

Situated on the Ayrshire coast, 13 miles south of Ayr. The property is now owned by the National Trust for Scotland and is open to the public. The existing castle was built from 1777 onwards by Robert Adam for the 10th Earl of Cassilis. It was built on the site of an ancient stronghold of the Kennedy family. Culzean is referred to as *'Colean'* in the poem *HALLOWE'EN* — *'Or for Colean the rout it ta'en.'*

CUMNOCK

Situated at the junction of the A76 Mauchline/Dumfries Road and the A70 Ayr/Muirkirk Road. The poet was very familiar with Cumnock and district, passing through regularly on his journeys between Mossgiel and Ellisland. The town was referred to in the poem *DEATH AND DOCTOR HORNBOOK* — *'The rising moon began to glowre, The distant Cumnock Hills out-owre.'* In a note to a suppressed stanza of the poem *THE VISION*, the poet indicated that the following line refers to Cumnock — *'Where Lugar leaves his moorland plaid.'*

Anne Rankine, later Mrs Merry, and probably the *'Annie'* of the song

THE RIGS OF BARLEY, lived in the town after her marriage and is buried in the old cemetery.

William Simson, friend and fellow poet of Burns was appointed school master at Cumnock in 1788, having previously been School Master at Ochiltree. He is buried in Cumnock Old Cemetery, near Anne Rankine.

Also see: Adamhill Farm; Dumfries House; Garallan; Logan House; South Auchenbrain Farm.

CUNNINGHAME

An ancient division of Ayrshire, being that part of the county north of the River Irvine. Kyle and Carrick are the other ancient divisions of the county. Cunninghame was referred to in the cantata *LOVE AND LIBERTY*, better known as *THE JOLLY BEGGARS* — *'Till I met my old boy in a Cunningham Fair.'* It was also referred to in a letter dated 17 July, 1787 from Burns to Mrs Dunlop of Dunlop — 'The farther corners of Cunningham, a place I little know.'

An entry by the poet in his first Common-Place Book, dated August, 1784, referred to Cunninghame, Kyle and Carrick — 'My dear native country, the ancient bailieries of Kyle, Carrick and Cunninghame. We have never had one Scotch poet of any eminence, to make the fertile banks of Irvine, the romantic woodlands and sequestered scenes on Ayr, and the healthy, mountainous source and winding sweep of Doon, emulate Tay, Forth, Ettrick and Tweed.'

Also see: Carrick; Kyle.

DALFRAM   Map Ref. 655 267

The house is no longer extant. It was situated on the south side of the B743 Muirkirk/Sorn Road, 2½ miles west of Muirkirk. It was the birthplace in 1727 and home of John Lapraik, Ayrshire ryhmer and an acquaintance of Burns; he was addressed in the three *EPISTLES TO J. LAPRAIK*. Although generally described as being from Dalfram, he was the farmer at Laigh Dalfram Farm, the site of which is marked by a cairn on the north bank of the River Ayr, about 100 yards south-east of Townhead Farm on the Muirkirk/Sorn Road. The cairn was erected in 1914 by the Lapraik Burns Club of Muirkirk.

As a result of having lost money in the collapse of the Ayr Bank in 1772, Lapraik moved from Laigh Dalfram to Muirsmill, then to Netherwood, back to Muirsmill, and to Nether Wellwood, all in the same area of Muirkirk Parish, and latterly into Muirkirk village. He is buried in Muirkirk kirkyard.

Lapraik's wife was Margaret Rankine, sister of John Rankine of Adamhill Farm, Tarbolton — 'rough, rude, ready-witted Rankine' — and an aunt of Anne Rankine, who was probably *'Annie'* of the song *THE RIGS OF BARLEY*. It may have been through this connection that Burns and Lapraik first knew of each other.

Tradition maintains that Burns was at a 'rockin' (social evening) in Mauchline when he heard a song being sung which appealed to him. On enquiring about the song he was told that it was by a man, Lapraik, from Muirkirk.

In a copy of Johnson's Musical Museum presented by Burns to Captain Riddell of Glenriddell, Dumfries, the poet made the following footnote to the song *WHEN I UPON THY BOSOM LEAN* — 'this song was the work of a very worthy, facetious old fellow, John Lapraik, of Dalfram, near Muirkirk. He has often told me that he composed this song one day when his wife had been fretting over their misfortunes.'

Also see: Adamhill Farm; Muirkirk; Muirsmill.

DALJARROCK HOUSE   Map Ref. 188 881

Situated one mile west of the A714 Girvan/Newton Stewart Road, 2 miles north of Pinwherry. The house is still occupied. It was the home of Robert Kennedy, father-in-law of Gavin Hamilton, the poet's friend and patron in

Mauchline. Kennedy's daughter, Peggy Kennedy, is the heroine of the poem *YOUNG PEGGY — 'Young Peggy blooms our boniest lass.'*

DALRYMPLE

Situated on the B742 Maybole/Coylton Road, 5 miles north of Maybole, and on the banks of the River Doon. It is the village nearest to the farm of Mount Oliphant where the poet lived from 7 to 18 years of age. In 1772, when Burns was 13 years old, he attended Dalrymple Parish School. Robert and his brother Gilbert could not both be spared from the work of Mount Oliphant, so for one term they attended on alternate weeks to improve their writing.

The site of the school is now occupied by the White Horse Hotel.

DALSANGAN MILL   Map Ref. 480 307

Now Dalsangan Farm, it is situated on the Crosshands/Fiveways Road, about 400 yards north of the B744 Crosshands/Largie Toll Road. The ancient mill was referred to as a working mill as early as 1205. It was a meal mill until the mid-19th century and tradition maintains that it was the mill used by Burns while he was at Mossgiel Farm. Not only was it the mill nearest to Mossgiel, the farm was probably thirled to it through the Earls of Loudoun. The miller was called Morton.

The water for Dalsangan Mill came from Loch Brown which lay in the depression west of the A76 Kilmarnock/Mauchline Road and south of the B744 Crosshands/Largie Toll Road. The loch was drained for the construction of the Kilmarnock/Dumfries railway line about 1847

Tradition maintains that Burns played curling on the loch and that Tam Samson of Kilmarnock joined him occasionally to go shooting on its shores.

Also see: Mossgiel Farm; Tam Samson's House.

DALWHATSWOOD   Map Ref. 542 381

Situated in Cemetery Road, Newmilns, almost a mile north of Main Street. It was formerly spelled Dalquhatswood. It was the home of John Arnot who subscribed to the first Edinburgh Edition of the poet's works and to whom the poet wrote one letter, post-dated as 'about the latter end of 1785.' In the Glenriddell Manuscript, the poet described Arnot as 'one of the most accomplished sons of men I ever met with — Alas! Had he been equally prudent.' There is no other reference to Arnot in the works of Burns. It is not known where or when the men became acquainted.

DAMHOUSE OF ARDLOCHAN   Map Ref. 221 088

Situated on the north end of Maidenhead Bay, a half mile north of Maidens village. Hugh Brown, miller, designated as of Ardlochan Mill or Damhouse of Ardlochan, is thought to have been the model for the *'miller'* of the poem *TAM O'SHANTER — 'That ilka medler wi' the miller, Thou sat as lang as thou had siller.'*

Damhouse of Ardlochan is still occupied. The mill, which was between the house and the shore, is no longer extant but the course of the lade and other features can be identified. It was the mill nearest to Shanter Farm and is certain to have been used by Douglas Graham, model for *'Tam'* in the poem *TAM O'SHANTER.*

Hugh Brown was related to the poet's mother and the poet probably visited him while in the area.

Douglas Graham of Shanter also farmed Laigh Park Farm, neighbouring Ballochneil Farm and Mill, Kirkoswald, and another tradition maintains that Robert Niven the Ballochneil miller was the model for the miller of the poem *TAM O'SHANTER.* Burns lodged at Ballochneil in 1775 while attending Hugh Rodger's school, Kirkoswald.

Also see: Ardlochan; Ballochneil Farm and Mill; Laigh Park Farm; Maidens; Shanter Farm.

**Cunningham Street, Tarbolton, circa 1910
with Doctor Hornbook's House third from the right.**

DOCTOR HORNBOOK'S HOUSE AND SCHOOL   Map Ref. 431 273

John Wilson, immortalised by Burns as *'Doctor Hornbook'* in the poem *DEATH AND DOCTOR HORNBOOK*, was school master at Tarbolton from 1781 to 1790. He was also session clerk of the church and secretary of Lodge St. James Tarbolton. Before he moved to Tarbolton, Wilson had been schoolmaster at Craigie, near the poet's home at Lochlea and Burns probably knew him or at least knew of him at that time. John Wilson's house is still inhabited. He lived in either No. 20 or No. 22 Cunningham Street, Tarbolton; the houses are semi-detached and it is not known for certain which one he occupied. They are now single storey houses with slated roofs but were originally of two storeys with thatched roofs. He sold 'remedies' from his home, advertising his services in a ground floor window.

The school in which Wilson taught is no longer extant. It stood on the south side of Cunningham Street, a few yards west of Wilson's house, and on the west side of what is now the vehicle entrance to Tarbolton Church and cemetery.

It has been said that the poem *DEATH AND DOCTOR HORNBOOK* brought such ridicule on John Wilson that he had to give up his job as school master, shut up 'shop' and leave Tarbolton. In fact, as fellow members of Lodge St. James and Wilson having been Lodge secretary when Burns was Depute Master, the two men were on good terms. In 1790, when Wilson decided to change his employment and leave Tarbolton, he wrote to Burns at Ellisland Farm, Dumfries. By then Burns was famous and Wilson sought his advice and assistance in obtaining a clerical post in Edinburgh. In a letter dated 11 September, 1790, the poet sent a very kindly worded reply, advising against the post but enclosing a reference to a lawyer in Edinburgh. Wilson accepted the advice and moved to Glasgow where he worked as a schoolteacher. He became session clerk of Gorbals Parish Church and is buried in Gorbals kirkyard.

Also see: Freemasonry; Johnie Ged's Hole; Tarbolton.

DOONHOLM HOUSE   Map Ref. 338 175
Situated south of Doonholm Road, Alloway and west of the A77Ayr/
Maybole Road. The house is still occupied. It was the home of Doctor William
Ferguson, Provost of Ayr. The poet's father, Willliam Burnes, worked as head
gardener at Doonholm. He had previously worked at the neighbouring Doonside
House.

Doctor Ferguson owned Mount Oliphant Farm and in November, 1765
leased it to William Burnes as from Whitsun, 1766. He also lent the poet's father
£100 to help him to stock the farm.

Doonholm was later the home of John Hunter, an Ayr lawyer who was
probably the gentleman referred to in the poem *EPITAPH FOR J.H.*
Also see: Ayr Auld Kirk; Mount Oliphant Farm; Doonside House.

DOON RIVER   Map Ref. 324 195
The river flows generally west through Ayrshire and enters the Firth of
Clyde 2 miles south of Ayr town centre, at the Map Reference shown. The river
is close to Burns Cottage and Mount Oliphant. Until he moved to Lochlea in
1777, aged 18 years, the poet must have been very familiar with the banks and
braes, holms and woods of its lower reaches.

There are numerous references to the river in the poet's works, the most
famous being in the versions of the song *THE BANKS O' DOON* — '*Ye banks and
braes o' bonie Doon, How can ye bloom sae fresh and fair?*' It is also famed for its
place in the poem *TAM O'SHANTER* — '*Before him Doon pours all his floods.*'

DOONSIDE HOUSE   Map Ref. 335 176
The house is no longer extant. It was situated on the south bank of the
River Doon, east of the B7024 Ayr/Maybole Road. It was the home of John
Crawford, who employed the poet's father, William Burnes, as a gardener. About
1752, 2 years after he came to Ayrshire from the east of Scotland, during which
time he had worked at Fairlie House, Dundonald, William Burnes entered
employment at Doonside.
Also see: Doonside Mill; Fairlie House; Doonholm House.

DOONSIDE MILL   Map Ref. 334 177
Situated on the north bank of the River Doon, a few hundred yards east of
Old Doon Bridge. Although originally called Doonside Mill, it is known as the
Dutch Mill. Even in 1754, when the lands of Alloway were feued off by public
roup, it was referred to as the Dutch Mill.

About 1752, the poet's father, William Burnes, moved to Alloway from
Fairlie House, Dundonald, and took up employment as a landscape gardener at
Doonside House and later Doonholm House. Local legend maintains that from
1752 until he was married and set up home in New Gardens (Burns Cottage) in
December, 1757, he lodged at Doonside Mill, although this can not be verified.

Legend also maintains that the only 'public' clock in the area was on a
building on Mill Brae, above the Mill, and that William Burnes was in the habit of
walking up the brae to see the time on the clock.
Also see: Doonholm House; Doonside House.

DOUGLASTON
Douglas Graham of Shanter Farm, model for '*Tam*' in the poem *TAM
O'SHANTER*, was born at Douglaston Farm. No farm of that name exists at
present but part of the village of Maidens retains the name Douglaston. In
Armstrong's 1775 Map of Ayrshire, the name Douglaston is shown in the area
now occupied by Maidens. The name Maidens would be unknown to Burns; it is
derived from twin rocks on the shore and did not appear on a map until 1828.

William Sloan, referred to as '*Haverel Will*' in the poem *HALLOWE'EN*, was

born at Douglaston in December, 1758. On the recommendation of the poet's uncle, Samuel Broun, he was employed as a gaudsman at Mossgiel. He returned to Kirkoswald Parish and was apprenticed as a shoemaker with John Davidson, the model for *Souter Johnie* in the poem *TAM O'SHANTER*. Sloan eventually settled in Dalmellington.
Also see: Ardlochan; Damhouse of Ardlochan; Glenfoot; Kirkoswald; Maidens; Shanter Farm; The Cellars.

DOURA FARM   Map Ref. 447 305
Situated a half mile south of the A719 Ayr/Galston Road, at a part 2½ miles east of the B730 Dundonald/Tarbolton Road. It is a neighbouring farm to Lochlea and was said by the Rev. Charles Rodgers in his Books of Burns to have been the home of Agnes Fleming.
The poet's brother, Gilbert Burns said that Agnes Fleming lived at Coldcothill Farm, a neighbouring farm to Doura and that she was the heroine of the song *MY NANIE, O*'.
The Ayrshire Register of Sasines shows that when the Burnes family lived in Lochlea, a family called Steven lived in Coldcothill. It also shows that one John Fleming was tenant of Doura. It is thought that Agnes Fleming's home was at Doura and that she worked at Coldcothill.
Other girls are also said to have been the heroine of the song. The poet gave no indication of the girl he had in mind.
Also see: Coldcothill Farm; Girvan River; Kirkoswald; Lugar River; Minnybae Farm; Peggy Thomson's House; Pinvalley; Ship Inn; Stinchar River.

DRUKKEN STEPS   Map Ref. 329 404
The Drukken Steps were situated on the Red Burn in Eglinton Estate, between Irvine and Kilwinning, at the Map Reference shown. The site is now covered by the Irvine by-pass dual carriageway. The ancient name of the site was St. Bryde's Well. In 1927 a plaque was placed near the Drukken Steps to commemorate the area as a favourite walk of Burns and his friend Richard Brown during the period when the poet was living in Irvine. In a letter to Brown dated 30 December, 1787 the poet wrote — 'Do you recollect a Sunday we spent in Eglinton Woods?'
In 1976, on the construction of Irvine by-pass, Irvine Burns Club had the plaque re-located on a cairn in Mackinnon Terrace, Irvine, 700 yards south-east of its original position at the Drukken Steps.
Also see: Eglinton; Irvine.

DUCAT STREAM   Map Ref. 341 218
An ancient ford on the River Ayr, in the vicinity of the modern Turner's Bridge, Ayr. It can still be detected at low tide, especially when the river is also low. It is referred to in the poem *THE BRIGS OF AYR* — *'There's men o' taste would tak the Ducat Stream.'* In a note to the poem, Burns indicated that it was 'a noted ford, just above the Auld Brig.'
The name of the ford is probably derived from the 'Doo-Cot' or 'Dove-Cot' of the ancient priory which stood on the site of the Auld Kirk of Ayr.

DUMFRIES HOUSE   Map Ref. 542 204
Situated north of the A70 Ayr/Cumnock Road, one mile west of Cumnock. The house was built between 1754 and 1759 and is still extant. John Kennedy, friend and correspondent of Burns, was factor to the Earl of Dumfries at Dumfries House. He was related to Gavin Hamilton, the poet's Mauchline friend and patron. Burns sent Kennedy copies of his poems and Kennedy was probably the first person to be shown the poem *TO A MOUNTAIN DAISY*. John Kennedy was the subject of the poems *LINES TO JOHN KENNEDY* and *TO JOHN KENNEDY*.

DUMFRIES HOUSE. In the second postscript (last stanza) of the poem *THE KIRKS ALARM,* he was referred to as *'Factor John'* — *'Factor John! Factor John! Whom the Lord made alone, And ne'er made another thy peer.'*
The poet's father-in-law, James Armour, is reputed to have been engaged in the building of Dumfries House.

DUNASKIN
Situated on the A713 Ayr/Dalmellington Road, about 2½ miles west of Dalmellington. It is now synonymous with the village of Waterside. In the poem *TO MR McADAM OF CRAIGENGILLAN* Burns referred to Mr McAdam's son, Quinton McAdam as — *'young Dunaskin's laird.'* Together with Barbeth, Straiton and Dalmellington, Dunaskin formed the estate of Mr McAdam.
Also see: Craigengillan House.

DUNDONALD
Situated on the B730 Irvine/Tarbolton Road, at its junction with the A759 Troon/Kilmarnock Road. Burns must have been familiar with the village as he had to pass through it on his journeys between Lochlea and Irvine. In 1786, when Jean Armour's father took out a warrant against him, Burns hid out near Old Rome in Dundonald Parish.
The Rev. Dr. Robert Duncan, *'Duncan Deep'* of the poem *THE TWA HERDS* was minister of Dundonald from 1783 until his death in 1815. He is buried in Dundonald kirkyard. The present church was built on the site of the previous church in 1803.
The Rev. Dr. Thomas Burns, the poet's nephew, while minister of Monkton was also in charge of Dundonald and ran the church with the assistance of a probationary minister.
When the poet's father, William Burnes, moved to Ayrshire from the east of Scotland, he lived and worked at Fairlie House in Dundonald Parish. On 26 November, 1752, Dundonald Parish Church Session gave him a character reference and verified that he had attended 'The Lord's Supper' in the church.
Also see: Fairlie House; Monkton; Old Rome.

Sandgate, Ayr with the Tolbooth Steeple
circa 1820

DUNGEON CLOCK
Map Ref. 337 220

The clock was on the steeple of Ayr Tolbooth or town jail which stood in the middle of Sandgate between Academy Street and Cathcart Street. A plaque on the wall of the Registry Office, Sandgate indicates the site of the Tolbooth. The building and its clock were removed in 1826. The dungeon-clock was referred to in the poem *THE BRIGS OF AYR* — *'The drowsy dungeon-clock had numbered two.'*

John Kennedy, described as keeper of the dungeon-clock, is amongst those listed as associates of Burns who are buried in Ayr Auld Kirkyard. Nothing further is known about him.

DUNLOP HOUSE
Map Ref. 427 494

Situated on the 'C' class road from Dunlop to Neilston, one mile east of Dunlop. The original house is no longer extant, the present one having been built in 1834. It was the home of Mrs Frances Dunlop of Dunlop, patron and friend of Burns. They corresponded regularly over many years and the poet visited the house on at least 5 occasions, staying overnight on 3 visits.

MRS. FRANCES DUNLOP

In 1786, Mrs Dunlop was given a copy of the poem *THE COTTER'S SATURDAY NIGHT* and was so taken with it that she wished to read more of its author's work. She sent a messenger to Mossgiel with a letter for Burns, asking him to send her half a dozen copies of his poems (Kilmarnock Edition) and inviting him to visit her home. Thus started a friendship and regular correspondence which was to last for the rest of the poet's life, except for a period of estrangement when Mrs Dunlop took offence at the content of a letter and broke off the exchange of letters. In a letter to Mrs Dunlop dated 26 October, 1788, Burns wrote of his intention to visit Dunlop Cow Fair at Hallowe'en.

When Burns and Jean Armour were married and moving into Ellisland Farm, Dumfries, Mrs Dunlop's son, Major Andrew Dunlop gave them a present of a cow. Also see: Craigie Village.

EGLINTON
Map Ref. 324 422

Eglinton castle has been almost completely demolished and the estate largely split up. The remnants of the castle are at the Map Reference shown, east of the A737 Irvine/Kilwinning Road, 2 miles north of Irvine town centre. It was the seat of the Montgomeries, Earls of Eglinton and Winton.

Colonel Hugh Montgomerie was referred to in the poem *THE AUTHOR'S EARNEST CRY AND PRAYER* as '*Sodger Hugh*'. Archibald Montgomerie, 11th Earl, subscribed for 42 copies of the poet's first Edinburgh Edition and Burns replied to the Earl's subscription enquiry in a letter dated 11 January, 1787.

When Burns was in Irvine, Eglinton estate was heavily wooded. In a letter dated 30 December, 1787 to his sailor friend, Richard Brown, the poet recalled their time together in Irvine and wrote — '*Do you recollect a Sunday we spent together in Eglinton Woods...?*' The woods in which they walked were probably on the site of the modern Castlepark housing estate. A cairn and plaque in Mackinnon Terrace, Irvine commemorate the favourite walk of Burns and Brown. Also see: Drukken Steps; Irvine.

ELBOW TAVERN   Map Ref. 497 274
The tavern was situated at the west end of The Knowe, Mauchline on its south side. A lane, on the same line as an existing lane, ran from Kilmarnock Road to The Knowe and on to Loudoun Street. The bend in the lane at The Knowe was known as The Elbow and as that was where the tavern sat, so arose the name. Legend maintains that the tavern was conducted by an old sailor known locally as 'The Old Tar'.

Joseph Train, who was born at Gilmilnscroft, Sorn in 1779, and collected material on Burns from contemporaries of the poet, recorded the poet's close friend, John Richmond, as having said that Highland Mary Campbell was of low morals. Richmond claimed that while she was associating with Burns she was also the mistress of one of the Montgomerie family, a brother of the Earl of Eglinton. According to Richmond, the poet's friends warned him about Mary but he would not be convinced. One night the friends took Burns to the Elbow Tavern, knowing that Mary was in a back room with Montgomerie. Eventually, Mary emerged from the room and was jeered by the poet's friends. A few minutes later, Montgomerie came out of the back room and left the tavern. Burns was obviously upset at the time but, to the dismay of his friends, he continued his friendship with Mary a few days later. Richmond is quoted as having said that Burns returned to Mary, 'Like the dog to its vomit.'

It must also be recorded that a nephew of Richmond's said after his death that his uncle had been an inveterate liar.
Also see: Failford; Mauchline Burn; Stairaird; Richmond's House.

ENTERKINE   Map Ref. 423 237
Situated on the north bank of the River Ayr, one mile east of Annbank. The original house has been demolished and a new one built nearby. It was the home of William Cunningham of Annbank and Enterkine, son-in-law of the poet's patron, Mrs Stewart of Stair and Afton Lodge. Cunningham was referred to in the song *THE FETE CHAMPETRE* — '*Annbank, wha guessed the ladies' taste, H gies a Fete Champetre.*'

According to John McVie in his book Burns and Stair (1927), the event referred to as The Fete Champetre was probably held on the holm on the north bank of the River Ayr, immediately below the original Enterkine House. The purpose of the event was for Cunningham to introduce himself to the nobility of Ayrshire, although Burns implies that Cunningham intended to stand for election as a Member of Parliament and wished to ingratiate himself for that purpose.
Also see: Afton Lodge; Stair House.

FAIL   Map Ref. 421 287
A hamlet on the A719 Ayr/Galston Road, at its junction with the B730 Dundonald/Tarbolton Road. It is referred to in the poem *THE TARBOLTON LASSIES* — '*Gae doon by Faile, and taste the ale. And tak a look o' Mysie.*' There

is nothing to indicate the identity of 'Mysie'.
Also see: Lochlea Farm; Tarbolton.

Monument to the parting of Burns and Highland Mary

FAILFORD

Situated on the A758 Ayr/Mauchline Road, 2½ miles west of Mauchline. It is generally accepted as the scene of one of the most romantic incidents in the life of Robert Burns. In 1786, the poet had become estranged from Jean Armour over the breaking of their marriage arrangement when her parents found her to be pregnant by Burns and had their 'contract' defaced. Highland Mary Campbell worked as a nursery maid for Gavin Hamilton, the poet's friend and patron, and after breaking with Jean he began to associate with Mary. About the same time he had been offered a job in Jamaica and was preparing for his departure. He asked Mary to go with him to the West Indies as his wife. In May, 1786 Burns and Mary met for what proved to be the last time; she was leaving for her home in Argyll to make arrangements for her departure with Burns. The poet described the meeting in a letter to George Thomson, Song Collector, in October, 1792 — 'We met by appointment on the second Sunday of May, in a sequestered spot, by the Banks of Ayr, where we spent the day in taking farewell before she should embark for the West Highlands, to arrange matters for our projected change of life.' Mary died at Greenock and they never met again.

At their parting, Burns and Mary exchanged bibles as a token of their love, and possibly, betrothal. By old Scottish custom, the bibles would be exchanged across running water. The bible Burns gave to Mary is now on display in Burns Monument, Alloway. The bible given to Burns has not been traced.

A monument erected in 1921 on the west bank of the Fail Water near where it joins the River Ayr, at Failford, commemorates the parting. The location is generally accepted as the poet's 'sequestered spot.' Other locations said to have been the scene of the parting are Stairaird, a few hundred yards up the River Ayr from Failford, where the Mauchline Burn joins the River Ayr, and a wood near Kingencleugh, Mauchline, on the north bank of the River Ayr.

James Humphrey, subject of the poem ON A NOISY POLEMIC — 'Below thir stanes lie Jamie's banes' — spent most of his life in the vicinity of Failford. He was probably born in a cottage on West Cairngillan Farm, near the junction of the A758 Ayr/Mauchline Road and the B730 Tarbolton/Stair Road; the site is indicated by a clump of large trees in the field on the west side of the Tarbolton/ Stair Road, about 100 yards north of the Ayr/Mauchline Road. From the wording of the poem, Humphrey is known in Burns lore as 'the bletherin' bitch'. James Humphrey was a stone mason and did work at both Lochlea and Mossgiel Farms. Later in life he was Toll Keeper at Woodhead Toll on the Ayr/Mauchline Road, at its junction with the Failford/Largie Toll Road. The toll house is not extant. At an advanced age he moved into a trust house for the elderly in Failford. He is buried in Mauchline Kirkyard.

Also see: Gavin Hamilton's House; Kingencleugh; Mauchline Burn; Monuments, etc.; Stairaird; Tarbolton.

The River Fail where it joins the River Ayr at Failford

FAIL WATER   Map Ref. 459 262
    It joins the River Ayr from the north at Failford, 3 miles west of Mauchline, at the Map Reference shown. It is referred to in the poem *THE BRIGS OF AYR* — *'From where the Feal wild-woody coverts hide.'* The parting of Burns and Highland Mary Campbell is generally accepted as having been where the Fail Water joins the River Ayr at Failford.
Also see: Failford.

FAIRLIE HOUSE   Map Ref. 385 358
    Situated to the north of the A759 Troon/Kilmarnock Road, 1½ miles west of Gatehead. The original house is no longer extant. About 1750, the poet's father, William Burnes, moved from the east of Scotland to Ayrshire and took up employment as a gardener at Fairlie House, home of Alexander Fairlie of Fairlie. He worked at Fairlie for about 2 years before moving to Doonside, Alloway.

Fairlie was referred to in a suppressed stanza of the poem *POOR MAILIE'S ELEGY* — *'She was the flower o' Fairlie lambs.'* Alexander Fairlie was a well-known agricultural reformer and his 'Fairlie lambs' were renowned for their excellence.

The poet's uncle and aunt, James Allan and his wife, Jean Broun, lived in a cottage on Fairlie estate where James was employed as a carpenter. Jean Broun was a half-sister of the poet's mother, Agnes Broun. Their son Robert Allan worked at Mossgiel as a ploughman. James died in 1789 and Jean moved into Old Rome cottages on the Kilmarnock/Troon Road near Gatehead. She re-married an Adam Blair of Dundonald and died in 1821, aged 71 years.

In 1786, Jean Armour's father, James Armour, took out a warrant against Burns, hoping to get money to maintain Jean and the twins she was expecting by the poet. Burns went into hiding with his uncle and aunt at Fairlie.

Tradition in the area maintains that William Burnes met the poet's mother, Agnes Broun, while she was visiting her half-sister, Mrs Allan at Fairlie. In fact, whereas William Burnes was at Fairlie between 1750 and 1752, Mrs Allan was not born until 1750. She was 18 years younger than the poet's mother and only 7 years of age when William and Agnes were married.

Also see: Craigenton Farm; Dundonald; Old Rome.

FENWICK

Situated on the A77 Kilmarnock/Glasgow Road, 4 miles north of Kilmarnock. The village is referred to in the poem *THE ORDINATION* — *'As lately Fenwick, sair forfairn, Has proven to its ruin.'* This is a reference to the ordination of the Rev. William Boyd as pastor at Fenwick on 25 June, 1782, and the public disquiet and controversy aroused by the appointment.

FORD

Referred to in the poem *THE RONALDS OF THE BENNALS* — *'The Laird o' the Ford will straught on a board, if he canna see her at a' man.'* The location referred to can not be identified. There is no property called Ford in the vicinity of Bennals Farm. It may be an abbreviation of Failford or Failford House, both on the A758 Ayr/Mauchline Road. The close proximity of the River Ayr and its numerous ancient fords makes identification difficult.

Also see: Bennals Farm.

FREEMASONRY

Robert Burns was associated with the following Masonic Lodges in Ayrshire:—
1. Lodge St. David Tarbolton No. 174
   The poet was initiated into the Lodge on 4 July, 1781, aged 22 years. He was passed and raised on 1 October, 1781. This Lodge was disbanded in 1843 and re-constituted in Mauchline in 1877 as Lodge St. David (Tarbolton) Mauchline No. 133, which holds the original charter.
2. Lodge St. James Tarbolton Kilwinning No. 135
   This Lodge had amalgamated with Lodge St. David on 25 June, 1781. On 8 July, 1782 they broke away again and re-constituted Lodge St. James. Although he had been the first man initiated into the amalgamated Lodge, the poet left St. David's for St. James'. On 27 July, 1784 he was elected Depute Master, a post he held until 1788. As Depute Master he presided at many meetings of the Lodge.
3. Lodge Loudoun Kilwinning Newmilns No. 51
   The poet was made an Honorary Member of the Lodge at a meeting in the Loudoun Arms, Newmilns on 27 March, 1786. His friend and patron, Gavin Hamilton, Mauchline, then Right Worshipful Master, introduced

him to the Lodge. The minute of the meeting records — "John Morton, merchant in Newmilns, is answerable for Mr Robert Burns's admission money."

4. Lodge St. John Kilmarnock Kilwinning No. 24 (now No. 22)
    The poet was made an Honorary Member of the Lodge at a meeting on 26 October, 1786. The minute of the meeting records — "Robert Burns, poet in Mauchline, a member of St. James, Tarbolton, was made an Honorary Member of this Lodge, (signed) Will, Parker." The Lodge met in the Old Commercial Inn, Croft Street. 'Will. Parker' was Major William Parker, Assloss House, Kilmarnock, friend of Burns and Right Worshipful Master of the Lodge. The Masonic Song composed by Burns and sung by him at the meeting refers to the Kilmarnock Lodge and Major Parker — *'Ye sons of old Killie, assembled by Willie.'*

5. It is almost certain that during his stay in Irvine, as a new and enthusiastic Freemason, Burns would attend meetings of Lodge St. Andrew Irvine which were held in The Wheat Sheaf Inn, High Street.

FULLARTON HOUSE   Map Ref. 345 303
A mansion house which was situated on the eastern outskirts of Troon, one mile west of the A78 Ayr/Irvine Road. It was demolished a few years after the Second World War, except for an ancient courtyard that has been modernised. Fullarton was the home of Colonel William Fullarton who is referred to in the poem *THE VISION* — *'Hence Fullarton, the brave and young'* and as *'Brydon's brave ward.'*

After service in the army, Fullarton returned to his estate and became a noted agricultural reformer. In a treatise on agriculture he acknowledged his indebtedness to Burns for a method of dehorning cattle - 'Mr Robert Burns, whose general talents are no less conspicuous than the poetic powers which have done so much honour to the country of his birth.'

Fullarton visited Burns at Ellisland during 1791 and the poet wrote to him from Ellisland in a letter dated 3 October, 1791.

Legend in Troon maintains that Burns visited Colonel Fullarton at Fullarton House but this can not be substantiated. As he was able to give an accurate description of the location of Orangefield House, Prestwick in a suppressed stanza of the poem *THE VISION*, Burns may have visited his friend and patron James Dalrymple at Orangefield. If he did so, it is reasonable to suppose that he may also have visited the neighbouring estate of Fullarton at the same time. However, the matter is no more than conjecture.
Also see: Orangefield House.

GALSTON
Situated on the A71 Kilmarnock/Edinburgh Road, 5 miles east of Kilmarnock and on the banks of the River Irvine. The town is referred to in the poem *THE HOLY FAIR* — *'The rising sun, owre Galston muirs, Wi' glorious light was glintin.'* The muirs referred to lie south-east of Galston and Newmilns. Legend maintains that Burns composed the poem *THE FAREWELL* while trudging over the muir on his way home from Newmilns to Mossgiel.

The Rev. George Smith, Minister of Galston, was referred to in the poems *THE HOLY FAIR* — *'Smith opens out his cauld harangues'* and *THE TWA HERDS* — *'Forby turn-coats amang oursel, There's Smith for ane.'* Rev. Smith was also *'Cessnock-side'* of the poem *THE KIRK'S ALARM*. He was great grandfather of Robert Louis Stevenson. He is buried in the kirkyard.

John Rankine of Adamhill Farm, friend and confidant of Burns moved into Galston and lived in Old Manse Close. He died on 2 February, 1810 and is buried in Galston kirkyard.
Also see: Adamhill Farm; Barr Mill; Craig Mill; Milrig.

GARALLAN HOUSE   Map Ref. 549 183
    Situated on the B7046 Cumnock/Skares Road, 2 miles west of Cumnock.
The house has been greatly altered but is still occupied. It was the home of Doctor
Patrick Douglas, Surgeon in Ayr. Doctor Douglas owned an estate in Port
Antonio, Jamaica and offered Burns the post of book-keeper on the estate,
resulting in the poet arranging to sail to the West Indies on the ship 'Nancy' in
1786. After the success of the first edition of his poems, Burns was encouraged to
go to Edinburgh and he abandoned his plans to emigrate. Burns visited Doctor
Douglas on 13 August, 1786, probably at Garallan House. Doctor Douglas was
one of nine men who met in Burns Cottage, Alloway during the summer of 1801,
to pay tribute to the memory of Burns.
Also see: Burns Cottage.

GARPAL WATER   Map Ref. 682 263
    Joins the River Ayr from the south at the map reference shown, one mile
west of Muirkirk. The burn is referred to in the poem *THE BRIGS OF AYR* — '*Or
haunted Garpal draws his feeble source.*' In his notes to the poem, Burns wrote —
'The banks of Garpal Water is one of the few places in the west of Scotland where
those fancy-scaring beings, known by the name of Ghaists, still continue
pertinaciously to inhabit.'
    A woman called Tibbie Pagan lived in a cottage on the banks of the burn,
making a living by singing, song writing and running a sheebeen. It is often said
that she wrote the song Ca' The Yowes To The Knowes and that Burns heard the
song, liked it, improved it and gave us the song we know. In fact, Burns wrote to
George Thomson, song collector, in 1794 that he had heard the song sung by a
minister called Clunie.
    The poet knew the area well by passing through on his journeys between
Mauchline and Edinburgh and by his visits to John Lapraik at Muirsmill.
Also see: Dalfram; Muirsmill.

GAVIN HAMILTON'S HOUSE   Map Ref. 497 274
    Situated in Mauchline town centre, north of Loudoun Street and adjoining
Mauchline Castle on its west side. It is still occupied. The house was the home of
the poet's friend and patron, Gavin Hamilton, a lawyer in Mauchline, and the man
to whom Burns dedicated the Kilmarnock Edition of his poetry. Gavin Hamilton
leased Mossgiel Farm from the Earl of Loudoun and used the farmhouse as a
summer residence. When the poet's father, William Burnes, was engaged in
litigation with the owner of Lochlea Farm, Robert and his brother Gilbert
arranged secretly with Hamilton for the sub-lease of Mossgiel.
    In the compositions and correspondence of Burns, Hamilton features
prominently. He is addressed in the poems *TO GAVIN HAMILTON, ESQ.* and
EPITAPH FOR GAVIN HAMILTON. He is referred to in *HOLY WILLIE'S
PRAYER* and his character is described in complimentary fashion in the poem *TO
THE REV. JOHN McMATH.*
    Burns was a frequent visitor to Hamilton's home and one particular visit
deserves to be mentioned. He called in at the house on his way to church and
learned that Gavin Hamilton was suffering from gout and could not attend the
service. Hamilton challenged the poet, for a wager, to produce a poetic account of
the sermon, in no fewer than 4 stanzas, by the time he returned after the service.
The Rev. James Steven, a visiting minister, used as his text, Malachi Ch.IV, Verse
2 — 'And ye shall go forth, and grow up, as calves of the stall.' Burns responded to
the challenge and won the wager with what are now verses 2 to 5 of the poem
THE CALF. Doctor Mackenzie of Mauchline visited Hamilton while Burns was
there and asked for a copy of the poem. The poet sent a copy to the doctor
during the evening, by which time he had added the first and sixth verses to
complete the poem.

Gavin Hamilton's House flanked by Mauchline Kirk and Castle

Over several years, Gavin Hamilton was in dispute with the Rev. William Auld, Minister of Mauchline Parish Church and his church session over minor religious misdemeanours alleged against him. Burns supported him and brought derision on the minister and session with several satirical poems.

One traditional version of the marriage of Burns and Jean Armour maintains that the ceremony was performed by John Farquhar-Gray, Justice of the Peace, Gilmilnscroft, Sorn, in Gavin Hamilton's home or office. The exact location of Hamilton's office is unknown but it is thought to have been in Back Causeway (Castle Street) or in Loudoun Street.

Burns first met Highland Mary Campbell when she worked for Gavin Hamilton as a nursery maid. Mary was born in 1763, probably near Dunoon. She moved to Ayrshire to find work and her movements are not clear; speculation has placed her in Irvine and Dundonald as well as Mauchline. In 1785 she took up employment in Gavin Hamilton's home but her stay must have been short as by May, 1786 she is thought to have been working at Coilsfield House, near Tarbolton.

In 1786 the poet had become estranged from Jean Armour over the breaking of their marriage contract when her parents knew she was pregnant by Burns. By frequenting Gavin Hamilton's home, he obviously knew Mary Campbell and he appears to have begun to court her after his break-up with Jean. Burns and Mary parted by the River Ayr in May, 1786; he had asked her to accompany him to the West Indies and she had gone home to arrange for her departure. Mary died at Greenock before they met again.

Also see: Failford; Gilmilnscroft House; Kilwinning; Mauchline Castle; Morton's Ballroom; Ronald's Inn; Stairaird.

GIGRIEHILL

The exact location is now unknown. It was a small farmhouse situated between Millburn and Lochlea Farms in Tarbolton Parish. A tradition in

Tarbolton maintains that one Barbara Tweedie, wife of a weaver who lived at Gigriehill, claimed to have been the model for 'Willie Wastle's wife' of the poem called *WILLIE WASTLE* or *SIC A WIFE AS WILLIE HAD*. There is no evidence to support the tradition. The song was written about 1792, eight years after Burns left Lochlea.

It has also been claimed that the models for Willie Wastle and his wife lived near Ellisland, Dumfries, but if models for the couple and 'Linkumdoddie' of the song did exist — and they may have been imaginary — they are most likely to have been located near the River Tweed and Logan Water, as described in the song. Tradition in the latter area locates the site of 'Linkumdoddie' and identifies the persons concerned; this tradition is supported by the fact that when the song was written, the poet was familiar with the area.

Tarbolton Parish is sufficiently rich in associations with Burns to make pointless such imaginative conjecture. Such specious claims debase factual Burns lore.

GILMILNSCROFT HOUSE   Map Ref. 556 254

Situated one mile east of the B713 Sorn/Catrine Road, one mile south of Sorn. It was the home of John Farquhar-Gray, Justice of the Peace, who was the man most likely to have married Burns and Jean Armour in 1788, although it can not be verified. There is no record of where the ceremony was performed and various claims have been made. Joseph Train (1779 - 1852), Ayrshire Historian, whose father was employed by Farquhar-Gray and who lived at Sorn as a boy, said that the ceremony was conducted by Farquhar-Gray in Gavin Hamilton's lawyer's office in Mauchline. Mrs Alexander, daughter of John Richmond and Jenny Surgeoner, both close friends of Burns and Jean Armour, claimed that the marriage took place in Ronald's Inn, Mauchline; and another traditional version maintains that it was in Morton's Ballroom, Mauchline. It is unlikely that evidence will ever by produced to prove any of the versions. The poet knew John Farquhar-Gray. At a meeting of Lodge St. James Tarbolton, held in Mauchline on 25 July, 1787, and over which Burns presided in his capacity as Depute Master, Farquhar-Gray was made an Honorary Member.
Also see: Gavin Hamilton's House; Morton's Ballroom; Ronald's Inn.

GIRVAN RIVER   Map Ref. 181 982

The River flows south-west through south Ayrshire and enters the Firth of Clyde in Girvan, at the Map Reference shown. In all editions of his works up to and including 1794, Burns showed the first line of his song *MY NANIE, O* as — *'Beyond yon hills where Stinchar flows.'*

In a letter to George Thomson, song collector, in 1792 Burns wrote — 'The name of the river is horribly prosaic — I will alter it.' He then gave the choice of Girvan and Lugar. Thomson chose Lugar and so it has remained.

In the town of Girvan, tradition maintains that the heroine of the song was Nannie Brown, daughter of the innkeeper of the Ship Inn which stood on the west side on Old Street, a short distance south of the cemetery wall.
Also see: Coldcothill Farm; Doura Farm; Kirkoswald; Lugar River; Minnybae Farm; Pinvalley; Ship Inn; Stinchar River.

GLASGOW VENNEL   Map Ref. 324 388

Situated on the east side of Townhead, Irvine, about 300 yards south of The Cross. The Vennel was previously called Smiddy Bar. About mid-summer 1781, when Burns was 22 years of age, he went from Lochlea Farm to Irvine to learn flax dressing. In the popular account of the poet's sojourn in Irvine, he went into partnership in a flax dressing workshop in Glasgow Vennel with a relation of his mother called William Peacock and lodged in a house in the Vennel, a few doors from the workshop. Peacock turned out to be a scoundrel. At New Year, 1782, the heckling shop was accidentally destroyed by fire and after working in another workshop for a few weeks, the poet returned home to Lochlea in March, 1782. In a joint venture by Irvine Development Corporation and Cunninghame District Council, Glasgow Vennel has been beautifully restored and is now an attractive stop on the Burns Heritage Trail.

GLASGOW VENNEL
in the mid 19th century with the poet's lodging on the right

The flax heckling workshop in which the poet worked with Peacock has been restored; there is no doubt about its authenticity but there has been doubt as to whether it was ever destroyed by fire as said by Burns. The workshop now has an exhibition of flax heckling tools and an audio-visual display on the story of Burns in Irvine. The house adjoining the heckling shop facing on to Glasgow Vennel is thought to be on the site of Peacock's home; the original house on the site had been demolished and reconstructed before 1826. The premises are now a shop cum exhibition room. The recently restored house at No. 4 Glasgow Vennel is indicated as the house in which Burns lodged. When the poet was in Irvine, the house at No. 4 was called Temple Dean; its history is uncertain but either it, or possibly another on the site was badly damaged by fire on 13 September, 1925. The initials and date 'RB 1782' have been carved on a lintel in the house but the authenticity of the carving as the work of Burns can not be substantiated. There has been some doubt as to the house in which Burns lodged. It has been said that he lived in part of the heckling shop or in Peacock's home until they separated, but the tradition generally accepted is that he lodged in a room of the house at No. 4 Glasgow Vennel.

A restored building at No. 3 Glasgow Vennel is called The Buchanite Meeting House. The Buchanites were a quasi-religious group led by a Mrs Elspeth Buchan who settled in Irvine for about 2 years until assaulted by a riotous mob and officially expelled from the burgh by the magistrates in 1784. Burns gave an account of the Buchanites to his cousin, James Burness, Montrose, in a letter dated 3 August, 1784. A very attractive local girl called Jean Gardner with whom Burns had been friendly left Irvine with the Buchanites. Jean and her parents lived in the Seagate, probably in the second house on the right from High Street.

The house on the north corner of the junction of Glasgow Vennel and Townhead , now the Porthead Tavern, was the home of Provost Hamilton whose family befriended the poet while he was in Irvine. The Provost's son, later Doctor Hamilton of Irvine, not only subscribed to the poet's Kilmarnock Edition but stood surety with others to John Wilson, the printer, for the cost of its production.

Also see: Drukken Steps; Eglinton, Freemasonry; Irvine; Monuments; etc.; Museums, etc.

GLENBUCK VILLAGE   Map Ref. 750 295

Situated one mile north of the A70 Muirkirk/Douglas Road, 3 miles east of Muirkirk. The village, now almost completely demolished, was referred to in the poem THE BRIGS OF AYR — 'And from Glenbuck, down to the Ratton-key, Auld Ayr is just one lengthened, tumbling sea.' In his notes to the poem, Burns refers to Glenbuck as 'the source of the River Ayr.' In a letter to Mr W. Chalmers, Ayr, shortly after he had ridden from Mauchline to Edinburgh, and enclosing 2 poems, Burns wrote — 'I enclose you two poems which I have carded and spun since I passed Glenbuck.'

GLENCONNER FARM   Map Ref. 495 194

Situated one mile south of the A70 Ayr/Cumnock Road, about one mile west of Ochiltree. It was the home of John Tennant and his family. When the Burnes family lived at the cottage in Alloway and at Mount Oliphant Farm, the Tennant family were their neighbours and friends at Laigh Corton Farm. John Tennant is generally said to have been a witness to the baptism of Robert Burns. In fact, the witness may have been his cousin, also John Tennant, who was the blacksmith at Alloway and whose smiddy (smithy) adjoined the Burnes cottage. The blacksmith's wife is thought to have been the 'gossip' referred to in the song THERE WAS A LAD.

In Burns lore, John Tennant of Laigh Corton and Glenconner is often referred to as 'Auld Glen', from the poem EPISTLE TO JAMES TENNANT in which the poet called him — 'Guid auld Glen, the ace and wale of honest men.' Burns also expressed his high opinion of him in a letter to Mrs. McLehose (Clarinda) dated March, 1788 — 'a worthy intelligent farmer, my father's friend and my own.'

When the Tennant family moved from Laigh Corton, and John Tennant took over Glenconner, he also became Land Factor to the Duchess of Glencairn. The Duchess was the mother of James Cunningham, 14th Earl of Glencairn, the poet's patron and friend.

While preparing his work for publication in the Kilmarnock Edition, Burns took a manuscript copy to Glenconner and read it to the Tennant family for their opinions and approval. The family recalled the visit with great pleasure.

In 1787, when the poet was offered the tenancy of Ellisland Farm, Dumfries, he had John Tennant accompany him on an inspection of the property. Unfortunately Tennant advised him to accept.

All of the older members of the Tennant family were closely acquainted with Burns from childhood and he referred to each of them in the poem EPISTLE TO JAMES TENNANT:—

James —	the eldest son and the person to whom the poem was addressed. He was miller at Ochiltree Mill.
William —	he was ordained as a minister and became an army chaplain. In the poem he was 'Preacher Willie'.

Rev. Wm. TENNANT

JOHN TENNANT, Jnr.

CHARLES TENNANT

DAVID TENNANT

ALEXANDER TENNANT

John Jnr. —	he farmed Auchenbay Farm, Ochiltree and was referred to as 'Auchenbay'. He became a wealthy farmer and landowner. In 1773 he attended Ayr Grammar School with Burns and shared a bed with him while they were lodging with their school teacher, John Murdoch.
David —	he went to sea, rose to command a naval ship and lost his right hand in battle. He was offered and refused a knighthood. In the poem he was referred to as — 'The manly tar, my Mason-Billie'.
Charles —	As a young man he was sent to Kilbarchan to learn weaving. The poet referred to him as 'Wabster Charlie'. He patented a method of bleaching linen, set up the vast St. Rollox Chemical Works in Glasgow and became a very rich businessman. For almost 200 years his descendants have been amongst the most illustrious in the land; at present they include the Lords Glenconner and Crathorne and Baroness Elliot of Harwood.
Alexander —	referred to as 'Singing Sannock', he emigrated to Cape Town where one of his grandsons rose to be Speaker of The House of Assembly.
Agnes —	'auld aquaintance Nancy' of the poem. She married George Reid of Barquharrie Farm neighbouring Glenconner.
Katherine —	'cousin Kate' of the poem. She was John Tennant's niece.

The history of the Tennant family from the 17th century to the 1970s is recorded in the very interesting book Tennant's Stalk by Nancy (Tennant), Lady Crathorne.

Also see: Ayr Grammar School; Auchenbay Farm; Barquharrie Farm; Burns Cottage; Laigh Corton Farm; Ochiltree.

GLENFOOT   Map Ref. 222 078
The house is no longer extant. It was situated on the east side of the A719 Ayr/Turnberry Road, opposite Kingshill Cottage.

It was the home of John Davidson, the model for 'Souter Johnie' of the poem TAM O'SHANTER. Douglas Graham, model for 'Tam' of the poem, lived at the neighbouring Shanter Farm.

In 1785, John Davidson moved from Glenfoot to a cottage in Kirkoswald. The cottage is now owned by The National Trust for Scotland and open to the public as a museum.

John Davidson's wife, Ann Gillespie, worked for the poet's maternal grandfather, Gilbert Broun, at Craigenton Farm and assisted the poet's mother, Agnes Broun, to look after the family when Gilbert Broun's first wife died. Agnes Broun was only 10 years of age when her mother died.

As indicated by the name 'Souter Johnie', Davidson was a shoemaker. He travelled into Ayr on market days, in connection with his trade, and possible did so with his neighbour, Douglas Graham. As was the practice with farmers and traders on market days, a few 'drams' would be consumed before the journey home.

Davidson was well known for his quick answers and canny sayings. An anecdote traditionally told about him is that when he was asked what would happen if the day ever came when the craft of shoemaking might end he replied — 'my craft will continue as long as calves are born with heads and bairns are born barefooted'.

Also see: Auchenblane; Kirkoswald; Shanter Farm; Souter Johnie's Cottage.

GREENAN BRIDGE   Map Ref. 327 191

Now called Doonfoot Bridge, it is situated on the River Doon, a few hundred yards from its mouth and on the A719 Ayr/Dunure Road, 2 miles south of Ayr town centre. The present bridge was built in 1861.

Armstrong's 1775 Map of Ayrshire shows a road from Ayr to south-west Ayrshire on the line of the present A719 road.

Tradition maintains that the cottage and shop on the west side of the road, immediately north of the bridge, was built of stone from the original Greenan Bridge. This is borne out by a stone plaque set into the north gable of the shop which appears to be the mason's stone from the original bridge. The wording on the plaque is now almost illegible and all that can be read is — 'Masons Adam Smith and James Armour'. The full wording on the plaque was originally 'This Bridge of Greenan was built by the Earl of Cassillis, Anno. Dom. 1772 — Masons Adam Smith and James Armour.'

Tradition also maintains that the mason 'James Armour', who built the bridge of 1772, was James Armour of Mauchline, father of Jean Armour and father-in-law of Burns. Jean's father was a master mason and contractor who is thought to have been involved in building work at considerable distances from Mauchline, including Dumfries House, Cumnock; Skeldon House, Dalrymple; and several bridges throughout Ayrshire. The fact that the other mason at Greenan Bridge was called Adam Smith supports the tradition; James Armour's father-in-law (Jean's grandfather) was another Mauchline master mason called Adam Smith. Armour's eldest son was called Adam after his grandfather Smith.

By coincidence, the Burnes family were living at Mount Oliphant Farm, within 2 miles of Greenan Bridge when the poet's future father-in-law and grandfather-in-law were engaged on the building contract.

GREENFIELD AVENUE

The avenue runs parallel to the River Doon and links the A719 Ayr/Doonfoot Road with the B7024 Ayr/Maybole Road.

The poet's father, William Burnes, working under contract to Ayr Town Council, constructed the road now called Greenfield Avenue in 1755/56.

Ayr Town Council minutes for January 1756, recorded a payment of £12.10/— to William Burnes as an instalment of the total cost of £50 for the building of the road.

Also see: Alloway.

GREENOCK WATER   Map Ref. 628 269

It joins the River Ayr from the north at the Map Reference shown, adjacent to the B743 Sorn/Muirkirk Road, 5 miles west of Muirkirk.

The burn was referred to in the poem THE BRIGS OF AYR — 'Or where the Greenock winds his moorland course.'

Burns was familiar with the area by passing through on his journeys between Mauchline and Edinburgh and by having visited John Lapraik at Muirsmill.

Also see: Dalfram, Muirsmill.

HAUGH   Map Ref. 497 253

A hamlet situated on the River Ayr, 1½ miles south-west of Mauchline.

It is sometimes said to have been referred to by Burns in the first stanza of the poem MAN WAS MADE TO MOURN — 'One ev'ning as I wandered forth, Along the banks of Ayr.

The location referred to was Bridge Holm a few hundred yards down river from Haugh.

Also see: Bridge Holm.

HIGH KIRK, KILMARNOCK   Map Ref. 430 384

Situated between Wellington Street and Soulis Street, Kilmarnock.

The kirk was built in 1731. The main building is original, only the spire and outbuildings having been added.

Minister from 1764 to 1773 was the Rev. James Oliphant, who was referred to in the poem *THE ORDINATION* — *'But Oliphant aft made her yell'*.

From 1774 to 1800 the minister was the Rev. John Russell who was referred to as *'Black Russell'* in the poem *THE HOLY FAIR*, *'Wordy Russell'* in *THE TWA HERDS* and *'Rumble John'* in *THE KIRK'S ALARM*. In the poem *THE ORDINATION*, he was again referred to - *'An Russell sair misca'd her'*.

John Wilson, the Kilmarnock printer who printed the poet's Kilmarnock Edition, is buried in the kirkyard. Wilson had moved to Ayr in 1803 and, with his brother, Peter, started a newspaper, The Ayr Advertiser, which is still published. He died on 6 April, 1821 and was returned to Kilmarnock for burial.

Also see: Laigh Kirk; Star Inn Close; Kilmarnock.

HOGSTON FARM

HOGSTON FARM   Map Ref. 224 087

Situated a half mile north of Maidens village.

The farm was the home of Helen McTaggart, wife of Douglas Graham of Shanter Farm. Graham was the prototype of Tam O'Shanter in the poem of that name and Helen, the prototype of Kate of the poem.

Also see: Shanter Farm.

HURLFORD

Situated on the A71 Kilmarnock/Galston Road at its junction with the B7073 Kilmarnock/Mauchline Road.

Until the late 18th century, the village was called Whirlford, the name obviously arising from its location on the River Irvine.

Burns must have been familiar with the area, as the village was on his route from Mossgiel to Kilmarnock.

In his book The Ayrshire Hermit (Tammie Raeburn) and Hurlford (1875), M. Wilson quotes a contemporary of Burns as having said that the poet travelled from Mossgiel to collect coal at Norris Bank, 2 miles south of Hurlford.

The name Norris Bank has fallen into disuse; it was situated on the south bank of the River Cessnock, 200 yards east of the B7073 Hurlford/Mauchline

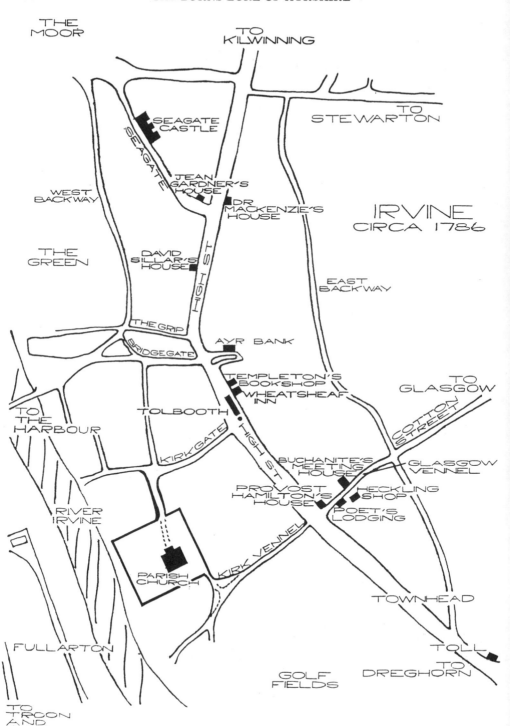

THE
MOOR

TO KILWINNING

TO STEWARTON

SEAGATE CASTLE

SEAGATE

JEAN GARDNER'S HOUSE

DR MACKENZIE'S HOUSE

IRVINE
CIRCA 1786

WEST BACKWAY

THE GREEN

DAVID SILLAR'S HOUSE

HIGH ST

EAST BACKWAY

THE GRIP

BRIDGEGATE

AYR BANK

TEMPLETON'S BOOKSHOP

WHEATSHEAF INN

TO GLASGOW

COTTON STREET

TO THE HARBOUR

TOLBOOTH

KIRKGATE

HIGH ST

BUCHANITE'S MEETING HOUSE

GLASGOW VENNEL

PROVOST HAMILTON'S HOUSE

HECKLING SHOP

POET'S LODGING

RIVER IRVINE

PARISH CHURCH

KIRK VENNEL

TOWNHEAD

FULLARTON

GOLF FIELDS

TOLL

TO DREGHORN

TO TROON AND AYR

Road, at Barleith. The contemporary said that Burns always had a book in his possession and read it during his journey.

Wilson's book also informs us that Burns was in the habit of visiting an inn which was situated on the west side of Mauchline Road, Hurlford. The innkeeper, James Aiton, was presented by Burns with a snuff box which was an item of interest for several years until eventually stolen.

HIGH STREET, IRVINE
before 1860 with the Tolbooth and Wheatsheaf Inn

IRVINE

Situated on the Ayrshire coast, at the mouth of the River Irvine, 15 miles north of Ayr.

About mid-summer 1781, when Burns was 22 years of age, he went from Lochlea to Irvine to learn flax dressing. The town was a busy seaport with a population larger than Kilmarnock or Ayr.

The popular version of the poet's sojourn in Irvine, supported by his own account, is that he went into partnership in a flax heckling workshop in Glasgow Vennel with a man related to his mother and called William Peacock. It is said that he lodged in a house in the Vennel, a few doors from the workshop. Peacock turned out to be a scoundrel. At New Year, 1782 the heckling shop was destroyed by fire and after working in other premises for a few weeks, the poet returned home to Lochlea in March, 1782. In fact, the subsequent history of the workshop in Glasgow Vennel casts doubts, not on its authenticity, but on its having been destroyed by fire.

There is additional information concerning the poet's stay in Irvine seldom taken into account although it deserves to be considered.

A man known as Robin Cummell, whose name was actually Robin Campbell (Cammell in the Ayrshire dialect), claimed to have known Burns in Irvine. Cummell was born in Kilwinning about 1745, worked at Eglinton Castle and died about 1840. He said that the poet lodged in High Street — "near the Gruip (Grip), just a wee before ye win to't comin' frae Kilwinning". Two Irvine contemporaries of Burns were recorded separately as saying that they witnessed the workshop the poet had moved into after splitting from Peacock, being destroyed by fire. Both said that the workshop destroyed had been in High Street, near the King's Arms Hotel. As the hotel is still at the High Street end of the lane called The Grip, the premises appear to be those described by Robin Cummell.

The true story of the poet's stay in Irvine probably includes parts of various accounts and it is certain that we will never know the story exactly. The only mistake of consequence would be to neglect any account totally in favour of another, as we are in danger of doing.

To return to the reminiscences of Robin Cummell, he said that he had met regularly with — "Burns; Richie Brown, the sailor; Keelivine, the writer (lawyer); and Tammie Struggles frae the Briggate" — in The Wheatsheaf Inn, High Street. Apart from Richard Brown, little is known of the men referred to.

Cummell's account of the poet in Irvine can be read in the book The Memorables of Robin Cummell (1913) by John Service.

Richard Brown was a sailor who became friendly with the poet in Irvine and it was he who first encouraged Burns to have his poems printed. They corresponded for many years thereafter and met occasionally. Burns claimed that Brown introduced him to 'the delights of women' but Brown refuted the claim many years later when he was a married man and a respected sea captain.

The only family in Irvine with whom Burns is known to have become closely acquainted was that of Provost Charles Hamilton whose home was on the north side of the junction of Glasgow Vennel and Townhead. The house is now part of the Porthead Tavern. The Provost's son, John, later Doctor Hamilton of Irvine, was friendly with Burns and in 1786 he did not only subscribe to the Kilmarnock Edition of the poet's work, he stood surety to John Wilson, the printer towards the costs.

In Irvine, Burns frequented James Templeton's bookshop in High Street. The site is now occupied by the Co-operative Society premises on the east side of High Street, south of the Cross. Templeton encouraged the poet's 'thirst' for reading; he subscribed later to the Kilmarnock Edition and acted as the poet's agent by collecting all of the subscriptions due in Irvine and forwarding them to Burns.

The Rev. James Richmond, parish minister when Burns was in Irvine, said later that the poet joined the Parish Church during his stay in the town but there is no church record to confirm his statement.

The poems WINTER — A DIRGE and A PRAYER UNDER THE PRESSURE OF VIOLENT ANGUISH were composed in Irvine.

David Sillar, the poet's Tarbolton friend and fellow-rhymer, moved to Irvine and eventually opened a shop close to the Tolbooth building which stood in the middle of High Street opposite Kirkgate. He also worked briefly as a school master in the town. His fortunes fluctuated; at one time he was lodged in the Tolbooth for debt but later he inherited between £30,00 and £40,000, and as a wealthy respected citizen became a member of Irvine Town Council. He owned a block of 4 houses on the west side of High Street, north of The Cross, on the site at No. 159 now occupied by the old Post Office building. In 1814 he bought a house in Kirkgatehead, at the corner of Hill Street. He died on 2 May, 1830 and is buried in the Parish kirkyard.

Doctor John Mackenzie, the poet's friend and family physician in Mauchline, moved to Irvine. The move was at the instance of the Earl of Eglinton whose personal physician the doctor became as well as having a practice in the town. The site of Doctor Mackenzie's house is on the east side of High Street, directly opposite the north side of Seagate. The building is no longer extant. The doctor had married Helen Miller, one of THE BELLES OF MAUCHLINE in the poem of that name. She died in Irvine and is buried in the Parish kirkyard.

Doctor Mackenzie and David Sillar were the first President and Vice-President of Irvine Burns Club. The Club has an excellent museum at 'Wellwood', Eglinton Street, Irvine. On 15 August, 1844 the poet's surviving sons, Major James and Colonel William Burns were entertained by Irvine Burns Club in the Kings Arms Hotel, High Street.

Also see: Eglinton; Freemasonry; Glasgow Vennel; Irvine River; Monuments etc.; Sun Inn.

IRVINE RIVER   Map Ref. 303 381

The river joins the Firth of Clyde in Irvine at the Map Reference shown.

It is referred to in the poems *EPISTLE TO WILLIAM SIMSON* — '*While Irwin, Lugar, Ayr and Doon, Naebody sings*' — and *THE VISION* — '*There well-fed Irwine stately thuds.*'

Burns knew much of the river by his familiarity with the Irvine valley towns; by having lived for a short time with his aunt and uncle, Jean and James Allan, at Fairlie Estate, Dundonald; and by his stay in Irvine.

Also see: Fairlie House; Galston; Irvine; Newmilns; Old Rome.

JOHNIE GED'S HOLE

Referred to in the poem *DEATH AND DOCTOR HORNBOOK* — '*Waes me for Johnie Ged's Hole now*' — its meaning is probably indicated in the next stanza as being the kirkyard.

Johnie Ged is generally said to have been the name of, or nickname for, the gravedigger. The Scottish National Dictionary shows it as a name for the personification of 'Death' but as 'Death' is being addressed in the stanza concerned, that meaning is not applicable. In Scots a 'Ged' is also a pike and a 'Ged's Hole' a pool frequented by a pike.

In Tarbolton, the scene of the poem, tradition maintains that at the time of Burns the gravedigger was one John Rodger who resided at Old House of Smithfield, known locally as Gedshall or Gedshole. According to the tradition, from the name of his home, Rodger was known as John(ie) Ged.

Old House of Smithfield is no longer extant. It was situated north of Smithfield Farm, Tarbolton and east of Tarbolton Mill, at Map Reference 436 276.

In the stanza in which reference is made to 'Johnie Ged's Hole', reference is also made to — '*His braw calf-ward whare gowans grew*'. The latter is also a reference to the kirkyard and relates to the custom of the time whereby the minister was entitled to the grazing of the kirkyard; if he did not take up his privilege, the grazing right passed to the gravedigger.

Also see: Doctor Hornbook's House and School; Tarbolton; Willie's Mill.

KELLY BURN   Map Ref. 194 684

The burn joins the Firth of Clyde at the Map Reference shown, between Skelmorlie and Wemyss Bay. It forms part of the boundary betweeen Ayrshire and Renfrewshire.

It is the subject of the poem *KELLY BURN BRAES*.

KILBIRNIE

Situated on the A760 Largs/Lochwinnoch Road, 10 miles east of Largs.

It is referred to in the poem *THE INVENTORY* — '*The fourth's a Highland Donald hastie, A d--n'd red-wud Kilbirnie blastie.*'

The reference was to 'an insane. unmanageable beast' bought by the poet at Kilbirnie Fair from a horse-dealer called William Kirkwood of Baillieston Farm, Kilbirnie. The farm is situated north of the A760 Kilbirnie/Largs Road on the outskirts of the town.

In a copy of Johnson's Musical Museum he presented to Captain Riddell of Dumfries, the poet wrote the following footnote to the song *A MOTHER'S LAMENT* — '*This beautiful tune is, I think, the happiest composition of that*

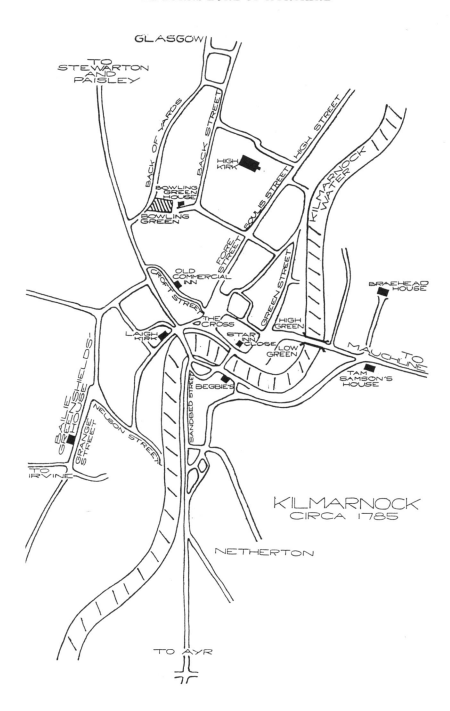

GLASGOW

TO STEWARTON AND PAISLEY

BACK OF YARDS

BACK STREET

HIGH KIRK

SOULIS STREET

HIGH STREET

KILMARNOCK WATER

BOWLING GREEN HOUSE

BOWLING GREEN

FORE STREET

OLD COMMERCIAL INN

CROFT STREET

GREEN STREET

BRAEHEAD HOUSE

THE CROSS

HIGH GREEN

LAIGH KIRK

STAR INN CLOSE

LOW GREEN

TO MAUCHLINE

BAILIE GREENSHIELDS HOUSE

NELSON STREET

GRANGE STREET

BEGBIE'S

SANDBED STREET

TAM SAMSON'S HOUSE

TO IRVINE

KILMARNOCK
CIRCA 1785

NETHERTON

TO AYR

bard-born genius, John Riddell, of the family of Glengarnock at Ayr'. Although the Riddells were an ancient family in the Kilbirnie area, John Riddell, a blind musician and composer was born in Ayr.

KILKERRAN HOUSE   Map Ref. 304 031
    Situated on the B7045 Crosshill/Girvan Road, 2 miles south of Crosshill.
    It was the home of Sir Adam Ferguson of Kilkerran, who was referred to in the poem *THE AUTHOR'S EARNEST CRY AND PRAYER — 'Thee, aith-detesting, chaste Kilkerran'.* In the *SECOND BALLAD ON MR HERON'S ELECTION*, Sir Adam was referred to as 'maiden Kilkerran'.
    The house is still occupied by the Ferguson family.

WATERLOO STREET, KILMARNOCK (now demolished)
The Kilmarnock Edition was printed in the first attic from the right

KILMARNOCK
    Situated at the junction of the A77 Ayr/Glasgow Road and the A71 Irvine/Edinburgh Road.
    The town holds an important place in Burns lore. The poet was familiar with the town and its surrounding area but the Auld Killie known by Burns was confined generally to an area within about 200 yards in radius from The Cross. It is still easy to envisage its picturesque location on the floor of the valley of the winding Kilmarnock Water with green and wooded slopes leading out of the valley on the roads to Glasgow, Mauchline and Irvine.
    Unfortunately, most of the locations associated with Burns have been obliterated by modern town centre developments.
    The town's most important association with Burns is unique; it was the place in which the fruits of his poetic genius first appeared in print. In the workshop of John Wilson, Printer, in Star Inn Close. the world renowned

Kilmarnock Edition was produced on 31 July, 1786. The printing workshop is no longer extant.

On the death of his father and the family's move to Mossgiel Farm, Mauchline, Burns became a farmer in his own right. Kilmarnock was his market and business town and he became a regular visitor. Through his wit and oustanding personality, he soon became a well known figure and was befriended by a group of leading citizens. The men he met in Bowling Green House, an inn adjacent to Kilmarnock Bowling Green, and who invited him to their homes, encouraged him to have his work printed and assisted in raising subscriptions for the Kilmarnock Edition.

The group of men who befriended Burns included Robert Muir, a wine merchant who was one year older than the poet and made a deep impression on him; John Goldie, businessman and religious theorist; Tam Samson, nurseryman and keen sportsman, his brother John Samson and nephew Charles Samson; Doctor William Mure, a local physician; the brothers William and Hugh Parker, landowner and banker; William Paterson, Town Clerk and businessman; Bailie Thomas Greenshield, brewer and Town Councillor; William Brown, merchant; and Sandy Patrick, Tam Samson's son-in-law and licensee of Bowling Green House.

The poet made many references to Kilmarnock in his works, the best known being:— the first line of the poem *TAM SAMSON'S ELEGY* — 'Has auld *Kilmarnock* seen the *Deil?*'; the first line of the poem *THE ORDINATION* — 'Kilmarnock wabsters fidge and claw'; and the first line of the poem *MASONIC SONG* — 'Ye sons of Auld Killie, assembled by Willie.'

Kilmarnock ministers featured prominently in the poet's works -- Rev. James Mackinlay, Rev. John Russell, Rev. James Oliphant, Rev. John Robertson and Rev. John Murtrie. Mackinlay and Robertson are buried in the kirkyard of Laigh Kirk, Kilmarnock.

On 21 June, 1784, the poet's brother, Gilbert Burns, was married to Jean Breckenridge of Kilmarnock in a first floor flat of a house at the corner of Waterloo Street and Green Street. The site is now under the town centre 'bus terminus. The poet travelled from Ellisland Farm, Dumfries to the wedding.

It is thought that Jean Breckenridge may have been a woman of property, albeit not impressive property. The Ayrshire Register of Sasines records that in April, 1781, Jean Breckenridge, daughter of James Breckenridge, merchant, Kilmarnock, inherited a tenement property in the town.

A Kilmarnock folk character who has gained a measure of immortality through Burns is Jean Glover. In a copy of Johnson's Musical Museum given by the poet to Captain Riddell of Glenriddell, Dumfries, he wrote the following footnote to the Scottish song O'er The Moor Amang The Heather which he had contributed to the collection — 'This song is the composition of a Jean Glover, a girl who was not only a wh---e but also a thief; and in one or other characters has visited most of the Correction Houses in the west. She was born I believe, in Kilmarnock. I took the song down from her singing as she was strolling through the country with a slight-of-hand blackguard.'

Jean Glover was born in Townhead, Kilmarnock on 31 October, 1758. The daughter of a weaver, she was good-looking and had a good singing voice. While singing in Kilmarnock taverns, she met and teamed-up with a man whose surname was Richard, 'the slight of-hand blackguard' referred to by Burns. Tradition maintains that the poet heard Jean singing in the Old Commercial Inn, Croft Street, Kilmarnock where meetings and social evenings of Lodge St. John Kilmarnock were held. An entry in the books of St. John's Lodge, dated September, 1793, shows — 'by cash — from Jean Glover's man, 7/—.' Jean died in Letterkelly, Ireland in 1811, aged 53 years.

A.B Todd antiquarian and poet, recorded having interviewed several old farmers who had known Burns and met him regularly at Kilmarnock market.

According to Todd, the farmers were unanimous and firm in their statements that they never heard the poet utter an oath, never saw him angry, and never saw him intoxicated.

The headquarters of the Burns Federation is in the Dick Institute, Elmbank Avenue, Kilmarnock. The Federation was established at Kilmarnock in 1885, and now has a world-wide membership of Burns clubs.

The many places in the town, of interest for their association with Burns, are dealt with separately.

Also see: Bailie Greenshield's House; Begbie's; Bowling Green House; Braehead House; Crookes's; Freemasonry (Kilmarnock); High Kirk; Laigh Kirk; Monuments etc; Museums etc.; Netherton; Riccarton; Star Inn Close; Tam Samson's House.

**JAMES CUNNINGHAM
14th EARL OF GLENCAIRN**

KILMAURS

Situated on the A735 Kilmarnock/Stewarton Road, 2 miles north of Kilmarnock.

In a letter ated 26 October, 1788 to Mrs Dunlop of Dunlop, Burns expressed his intention to attend Kilmaurs Cow Fair at Hallowe'en.

The Rev. Alexander Miller, 'Wee Miller' of the poem THE HOLY FAIR was minister of Kilmaurs Parish Church from 1788 to 1804 – 'Wee Miller niest, the guard relieves'. He is buried in the kirkyard.

Another Kilmaurs minister was referred to by the poet in a letter to Peggy Chalmers, dated 26 September, 1787 — 'the preaching cant of Father Smeaton, Whig-Minister at Kilmaurs'. The Rev. David Smeaton was Minister in the village from 1740 to about 1788.

James Cunningham, 14th Earl of Glencairn, friend and patron of the poet and subject of the poem LAMENT FOR JAMES, EARL OF GLENCAIRN, is buried in the Cunningham family aisle attached to Kilmaurs Parish Church. In a letter dated 10 March, 1791 to the Earl's factor, Alexander Dalziel, Burns asked to be informed of the arrangements for the Earl's funeral as he hoped to attend. There is no record of whether or not he did so.

It is thought that Alexander Dalziel, the factor, may have been responsible for drawing the Earl's attention to the poet's Kilmarnock Edition.

Also see: Mayville House.

KILWINNING
Situated at the junction of the A78 Irvine/Largs Road and the A737 Kilwinning/Dalry Road, 3 miles north of Irvine town centre.

The Rev. James Steven, minister of Kilwinning Parish Church from 1803 to 1828 was the minister whose sermon in Mauchline Parish Church inspired the poem *THE CALF*. When Burns heard him preach, Steven was 25 years of age and assistant minister at Ardrossan.

The story concerning the poem *THE CALF* is of interest. Burns was in the habit of calling on his Mauchline friend, Gavin Hamilton, on his way to Sunday morning service. On calling one Sunday, he learned that Hamilton was suffering from gout and unable to go to church. Hamilton challenged the poet, for a wager, to produce a poetic account of the sermon, in no fewer than 4 stanzas, by the time he returned after the service. The Rev. Steven used as his text, Malachi Ch.IV, Verse 2 – 'And ye shall go forth, and grow up, as calves of the stall.'

Burns responded to the challenge, and won the wager with what are now verses 2 to 5 of the poem *THE CALF*. Doctor Mackenzie, Mauchline visited Gavin Hamilton while Burns was there after the service and asked for a copy of the poem. The poet sent a copy to the Doctor during the evening, by which time he had completed the poem as we know it by adding verses one and six.

The Rev. Dr. William McGill, Minister of Ayr Auld Kirk, a friend to both the poet and his father, was assistant minister at Kilwinning before he moved to Ayr.

Peggy Orr, nursery maid at Stair House, who was an acquaintance of Burns and for a short time fiancee of the poet's friend, David Sillar, was born in Kilwinning where her father was a roads contractor.

Also see: Gavin Hamilton's House; Stair House.

KINGENCLEUGH   Map Ref. 503 255
In his book The Wanderer in Ayrshire, published in 1817, Hugh Campbell wrote of the ruined Kingencleugh Castle — 'A wood near these ruins, through which runs a rivulet, is said to be the place where Burns parted with Mary Campbell.'

The wood lies between Kingencleugh and the River Ayr at the map reference shown. It is known locally as the Lily Glen and is said to have been a favourite walk of Burns. Nearby are Ballochmyle House and the location where the poet saw Wilhelmina Alexander, heroine of the song *THE LASS O' BALLOCHMYLE*.

The claim of Kingencleugh area as the location of the parting is contradicted by the first stanza of the poem *HIGHLAND MARY* — *'Ye banks and braes and streams around, The castle o' Montgomery!....................... For there I took my last Farewell, O' my sweet Highland Mary.'*

Also see: Failford; Mauchline Burn; Stairaird.

KIRK—ALLOWAY   Map Ref. 332 180
Situated on the B7024 Ayr/Maybole Road, 300 yards north of the River Doon. It is thought that it was built about 1516. In 1691 it went out of regular use as a place of worship and became dilapidated. Between 1740 and 1752 it was reroofed and taken into use again as a place of worship and for some time as a school. By 1766 or earlier, it had become less than wind and waterproof and fell into disuse once more. When the antiquarian, Captain Grose, sketched the building in 1789, it was only partially roofed.

The road through Alloway to Old Doon Bridge was originally to the west of both Burns Cottage and Kirk-Alloway and the main entrance to the kirkyard was on the west wall, with no entrance on the east side.

KIRK-ALLOWAY with the poet's father's grave on the left

The ruined church was the setting of the witches' dance in the poem *TAM O'SHANTER* — '*Kirk-Alloway was drawing nigh, Where ghaists and houlets nightly cry*' and '*When glimmering thro' the groaning trees, Kirk-Alloway seem'd in a bleeze.*'

One tradition maintains that Burns was inspired by an incident at Kirk-Alloway when he created his story for the poem *TAM O'SHANTER*. A stray highland bullock had made its way into the ruined Kirk-Alloway, got stuck and, being without food or water, went half mad. A day or so later, a local woman passing the kirk looked in and saw a pair of horns, accompanied by a loud bellow. She fled in terror convinced that the Deil (Devil) was in the Auld Kirk, and pronounced her discovery to the world. Investigation showed the Deil to be the stray bullock. The story spread quickly through the district and could have stayed in the mind of the imaginative Burns who was about 9 years old at the time.

William Burnes, the poet's father, is buried in the kirkyard. He died in 1748 at Lochlea Farm, Tarbolton Parish, about 10 miles north-east of Alloway and his coffin was conveyed to Kirk-Alloway for burial, slung from two poles between two horses in tandem. The headstone on the grave is the third to have been erected, the first two having been mutilated by souvenir hunters. The poet's youngest sister, Isabella Burns Begg, and her daughters, Isabella and Agnes Begg, are also buried in the kirkyard.

David Watt, miller at Alloway Mill, and a school-fellow of Burns is accepted as having been the last person baptised in Kirk-Alloway. He died at Alloway Mill on 22 October, 1823, aged 68 years.

Also see: Alloway; Alloway Mill; Bridge House; Burns Cottage; Laigh Corton Farm; Lochlea Farm.

KIRKOSWALD

Situated on the A77 Maybole/Girvan Road, 4½ miles south of Maybole.

The village has many associations with Burns. His family background on his maternal side was all in Kirkoswald Parish.

KIRKOSWALD, circa 1900 - A Peggy Thomson's House. B Rodger's School. C Headstone for Burns's Grandparents. D Headstone for Douglas Graham and his wife. E Site of Hugh Rodger's House. F Headstone for Hugh Rodger.

In 1775, at 16 years of age, the poet spent one term at school in Kirkoswald, under Hugh Rodger, schoolmaster. While attending the school, he lodged at Ballochneil Farm, 2 miles south of the village.

Although the poem *TAM O'SHANTER* was set in Alloway, all of the main characters were modelled on people the poet had met in Kirkoswald Parish while staying at Ballochneil.

The present church was opened in 1777, so Burns must have attended the old church which is now a ruin. The following people associated with Burns are buried in the old kirkyard:— The poet's maternal great grandparents, John Broun and his wife Janet McGraen; the poet's maternal grandparents, Gilbert Broun and his wife Agnes Rennie; Douglas Graham and his wife Helen McTaggart,("*Tam*' and '*Kate*' of the poem *TAM O'SHANTER*); John Davidson (*'Souter Johnie'* of *TAM O'SHANTER*) and his wife Ann Gillespie who, as a girl, was employed by the poet's maternal grandfather, Gilbert Broun; Jean Kennedy *'Kirkton Jean'* of *TAM O'SHANTER*; and Hugh Rodger, Kirkoswald schoolmaster.

The following anecdotes relate to the poet's time in Kirkoswald. One day, while walking up the steep Kirk Brae in the village, the youthful Burns met the minister, The Rev. Matthew Biggar, coming down. The minister enquired as to where he was going and the poet replied — "As you see, Sir, I am going heavenwards" The minister was left to contemplate on his own direction of travel.

The minister's daughters met Burns and another boy in the village. As was his habit, the poet was walking with his head bowed and did not see the ladies approaching. One of the Misses Biggar jokingly chided him on his lack of attention to the fair sex, thereby missing the opportunity to look upon and talk with ladies. The poet's quick reply was to the effect that it was right for man to contemplate the earth from whence he was taken and for woman to look upon man from whence she was taken.

Elizabeth Biggar (1757 — 1838) married John Graham of Dalquhat Farm, Kirkoswald, nephew of Douglas Graham (Tam O'Shanter). Louisa Biggar (1761— 1846) married her father's successor, the Rev. James Inglis and it was he who recounted the anecdotes about Burns.

The many places of interest associated with the poet are dealt with separately.

Also see: Achmachalla; Ballochneil Farm; Laigh Dalquhat Farm; Laigh Park Farm; Minnybae Farm; Rodger's School; The Ladies' House; Souter Johnie's Cottage; Peggy Thomson's House.

KNOCKHASPIE'S LAND   Map Ref. 486 288

It is referred to in the song *HIGHLAND HARRY BACK AGAIN* — '*I wad gie a' Knockhaspie's Land, For Highland Harry back again*'.

The origin of the name is in doubt; Alan Cunningham, Burns biographer, wrote early in the 19th century that it was part of Mossgiel Farm and this is borne out by the fact that it is still the name of a large field on Mossgiel, two fields from the back of the steading.

In a copy of Johnson's Musical Museum given by the poet to Captain Riddell of Glenriddell, Dumfries, he wrote the following footnote to the song *HIGHLAND HARRY BACK AGAIN* — 'The oldest title I ever heard to this air, was the Highland Watch's Farewell to Ireland. The chorus I pickt up from an old woman in Dunblane; the rest of the song is mine'. As Knockhaspie's Land is referred to in the chorus, it could be implied that the name was in the original song collected by Burns, probably in 1787.

It is possible that the name was given to the field on Mossgiel some time after Burns wrote the song but it is thought to be unlikely.

Also see: Mossgiel Farm.

KNOCKSHINNOCH   Map Ref. 610 129

Situated south of the B741 New Cumnock/Dalmellington Road, one mile west of New Cumnock.

The exact location of Knockshinnoch House is not known. From its position on Armstrong's 1775 Map of Ayrshire, it was probably on the site occupied later by Knockshinnoch Colliery.

The poet's friend, John Logan, was designated as Laird of Knockshinnoch and the neighbouring property of Laight.

Also see: Laight.

KYLE

An ancient division of Ayrshire, being that part of the county between the Rivers Irvine and Doon. The other divisions are Carrick and Cunninghame.

The name is derived from Coil or Coilus, King of the Picts, whom legend maintains lived in Ayrshire in ancient times.

There are many references to Kyle in the works of Burns, the best known being in the song *THERE WAS A LAD* — '*There was a lad was born in Kyle*' — in which the poet wrote of his own birth.

Burns referred to Kyle as Coila in the poem *EPISTLE TO WILLIAM SIMSON* — '*We'll sing auld Coila's plains an' fells' and 'O' sweet are Coila's haughs and woods*'. In the poem *THE VISION*, Burns gave the name Coila to his poetic muse.

An entry by the poet in his First Commonplace Book, dated August, 1784, referred to Kyle, Carrick and Cunninghame — '*My dear native country, the ancient bailieries of Carrick, Kyle and Cunningham . . . . . . We have never had one Scotch Poet of any eminence, to make the fertile banks of Irvine, the romantic woodlands and sequestered scenes on Ayr, and the healthy, mountainous source and winding sweep of Doon, emulate Tay, Forth, Ettrick and Tweed*'.

Also see: Carrick; Cunninghame.

The 'AULD NICK' or 'CLOOTIE' Horn in 1985

LAIGH CORTON FARM   Map Ref. 352 178
      Situated on Corton Road, Ayr a half mile east of the A77 Ayr/Maybole
Road.
      A neighbouring property to Mount Oliphant, it was farmed by John
Tennant, a friend of both Burns and his father.
      John Tennant later moved to Glenconner Farm, Ochiltree. He is known in
Burns lore as 'auld Glen', derived from a reference to him by the poet in the
poem *EPISTLE TO JAMES TENNANT*, which was addressed to John Tennant's
son — 'guid auld Glen, The ace and wale of honest men'.
      It is generally said that John Tennant was a witness to the baptism of Burns.
In fact, the man shown as a witness was probably his cousin, also John Tennant,
blacksmith at Alloway, whose smiddy (smithy) neighboured the Burnes family
cottage. The smiddy operated as such until after the Second World War and the
dwelling at No. 6 Main Street, Alloway, is still called Smiddy Cottage. The
blacksmith's wife is reputed to have been a midwife at the poet's birth and the
'gossip' referred to in the song *THERE WAS A LAD* — 'The gossip keekit in his
loof.'
      John Tennant of Laigh Corton was one of the Alloway parents who joined
William Burnes, the poet's father, to bring John Murdoch, schoolteacher to
Alloway to open a school.
      A Tennant family tradition maintained that Burns recalled an incident at
Kirk-Alloway when creating his story for the poem *TAM O'SHANTER*. A stray
highland bullock had made its way into the ruinous Kirk-Alloway, got stuck and,
being without food or water, was half mad. A day or so later a local woman
passing the Kirk looked in and saw a pair of horns, accompanied by loud
bellowing. She fled in terror, convinced that the Deil (Devil) was in the auld kirk,
and pronounced her discover to the world. One of the Tennant boys of Laigh
Corton went to investigate and found the stray bullock. The story spread quickly
round the district and could have stayed in the mind of the imaginative Burns who
was about 9 years old at the time.

A sequel to the story was that when the bullock was being extricated, a horn was knocked off. The horn was retained by the Tennant family and later, complete with silver mounting, was given to the Ochiltree town crier for blowing as a horn for official duties. It was returned later to the Tennant family.
Also see: Auchenbay Farm; Barquharrie Farm; Glenconner Farm; Kirk Alloway.

LAIGH DALQUHAT FARM   Map Ref. 222 065
Situated on the A77 Maybole/Girvan Road, 2 miles south of Kirkoswald.
It was a neighbouring farm to Ballochneil where Burns lived with the Niven family while attending Kirkoswald school in 1775.
A man McTaggart, brother-in-law of Douglas Graham the model for Tam O'Shanter, farmed Laigh Dalquhat when Burns was at Ballochneil.
When Burns was in Kirkoswald, the minister was the Rev. Matthew Biggar. The minister's third eldest daughter, Elizabeth, married John Graham of Dalquhat Farm, nephew of Douglas Graham. She died in 1838, aged 82 years.
Also see: Ballochneil; Kirkoswald.

LAIGH KIRK

LAIGH KIRK   Map Ref. 428 379
Situated in Kilmarnock town centre, west of the Cross.
The church was extensively re-built on the same site in 1802 after a fall of plaster from the ceiling caused panic and 29 people were killed. The tower is all that remains of the original building.
The church is referred to in the poem THE ORDINATION — 'Swith! to the Laigh Kirk, ane an' a'.' THE ORDINATION was composed on the occasion of the Rev. James Mckinlay being ordained to the kirk in 1786.
The Rev. Mackinlay, Rev. John Robertson and Rev. John Murtrie, all referred to in THE ORDINATION were ministers of Laigh Kirk.
The Rev. Mackinlay, Rev. John Robertson and Tam Samson of the poems TAM SAMSON'S ELEGY and TAM SAMSON'S EPITATH, are buried close to each other in the kirkyard.

LAIGH PARK FARM

LAIGH PARK FARM   Map Ref. 223 062
    Situated east of the A77 Maybole/Girvan Road, 2 miles south of
Kirkoswald. The property is now called Park Farm.
    It was a neighbouring farm to Ballochneil Farm and Mill where Burns lodged
with the Niven family in 1775 while attending Rodger's school in Kirkoswald.
    Douglas Graham of Shanter Farm, Maidens, model for 'Tam' in the poem
'TAM O'SHANTER', also farmed Laigh Park and the poet must have met him
while living at Ballochneil. Tradition maintains that Douglas Graham died in the
existing Laigh Park farmhouse.
    Kate Steven or Stein, reputed to be a witch, lived in a cottage on Laigh
Park. She is said to have been the model for Nannie (Cutty Sark) of the poem
TAM O'SHANTER.
Also see: Ballochneil Farm; Park Farm; Shanter Farm.

LAIGHT   Map Ref. 612 117
    Situated in Glen Afton, New Cumnock, 1½ miles south of the town. The
house is still extant and inhabited.
    It was the home of the poet's friend, John Logan, described as Laird of
Laight, Afton and Knockshinnoch. Burns visited Laight and local tradition
maintains that it was after a visit that he returned to his lodging in an inn at New
Cumnock and composed the song SWEET AFTON.
    In a letter dated 14 October, 1788 from Ellisland to Jean Armour at
Mauchline, Burns wrote — 'You need not come on Sunday to meet me on the
road as I am engaged that day to dine with Mr. Logan at Laight.' On 23 October,
1788 he wrote to Mrs. Dunlop of Dunlop — 'I breakfasted this morning at Laight,
near New Cumnock.'
    The first reference to the poem THE KIRK'S ALARM was in a letter from
Burns to Logan, dated 7 August, 1789.
Also see: Afton River; Knockshinnoch; New Cumnock.

LANGLANDS FARM   Map Ref. 424 265
    Situated west of the B744 Tarbolton/Annbank Road, one mile south of
Tarbolton.

It was the home of John Reid whose wife was Jean Ronald of the poem *THE RONALDS OF THE BENNALS* — *'There's ain they ca' Jean, I'll warrant ye've seen, As bonnie a lass or as braw, man.'*

The poet's brother, Gilbert Burns, courted Jean Ronald briefly while he lived at Lochlea Farm.

Also see: Aikenbrae Farm; Bennals Farm.

LARGIESIDE   Map Ref. 467 294

The dwelling is no longer extant and its exact location is uncertain. An early 18th century map shows it on the east side of the B733 Tarbolton/Galston Road, about 150 yards north of Largie Toll but strong local tradition maintains that it was on the north side of the same road, about 100 yards east of Largie Toll, the site now occupied by a modern bungalow. Either way it was within a mile south of Lochlea Farm.

It was the home of Elizabeth Paton who was employed at Lochlea by the Burnes family and in 1785 had an illegitimate daughter by the poet. The child was called Elizabeth Burns; she was the subject of the poem *A POET'S WELCOME TO HIS LOVE-BEGOTTEN DAUGHTER* and was referred to as *'Dear-bought Bess'* in the poem *THE INVENTORY*.

Elizabeth Burns was reared by the poet's mother. She married one John Bishop of Polkemmet and had seven children. She is buried in Whitburn Cemetery.

In July, 1786 when Burns was preparing to emigrate to Jamaica, he signed a Deed of Assignment in favour of his brother Gilbert. All of his property, including the anticipated profits from the Kilmarnock Edition of his poems which was about to be published, was assigned to Gilbert who was pledged to care for and support Elizabeth Burns until she was 15 years old.

The Deed was drawn up by William Chalmers, an Ayr lawyer. Chalmers was courting a young lady and he asked the poet to write a poem to help him in his wooing. The result was the poem called *WILLIE CHALMERS* or *TO WILLIE CHALMERS' SWEETHEART*.

LARGS

Situated on the north Ayrshire coast, 35 miles north of Ayr.

The town is referred to in the poem *CALEDONIA — A BALLAD* — *'But brave Caledonia in vain they assail'd, as Largs well can witness and Loncartie tell'.*

The reference relates to the Battle of Largs in 1263 when King Alexander III of Scotland defeated King Haakon to end Norse domination of Scotland.

A Burns Garden, incorporating the flowers referred to by the poet in his poems, is located in Douglas Park, Irvine Road, Largs.

LEEZIE'S POOL

The pool is referred to in the 26th stanza of the poem *HALLOWE'EN*. The location described, if not imagined by the poet, is unknown.

Although the poem is generally accepted as having been set in the vicinity of Culzean and Kirkoswald, Ayrshire Archaeological and Natural History Society have suggested that much of the poem, including Leezie's pool, can be closely associated with Mount Oliphant.

The Society identify the pool described in the 24th stanza of the poem as being *'Whare three lairds' lands met at a burn'*, as a pool at the meeting place of the lands of Mount Oliphant, Broomberry and Pleasantfield.

It is also suggested by the Society that the characters *Rob* and *Nell (or Rab and Nelly)* in the poem refer to the poet and his first love, Nellie Kilpatrick, whom he met at Mount Oliphant; the burn of the 25th stanza is compared with several features of Riddicks Moss Burn; and the kiln to which Merran went in the 11th stanza is seen as disused lime kilns near Leezie's pool.

The verdict on the Society's detective work must be 'Not Proven' but the evidence is very plausible and worthy of consideration. When creating the atmosphere and setting the scene for his poem, the poet would certainly draw from the full width of his experience.

Volume 5 (Ayrshire At The Time Of Burns) of the Ayrshire Archaeological and Natural History Society's Collections describes the Society's research.

LEGLEN WOOD   Map Ref. 388 230
Situated one mile south of the A758 Ayr/Mauchline Road, 2½ miles east of Ayr town centre.

The woods are on the banks of the River Ayr and are said to have been a favourite haunt and hiding place of the Scottish patriot, William Wallace.

A cairn on the south bank of the river, and on the west side of the Auchencruive/Belston Road, commemorates the two patriots, Burns and Wallace.

In a letter dated 15 November, 1786 to Mrs. Dunlop of Dunlop, Burns described how as a boy, and already a fervent admirer of Wallace, he made a pilgrimage on a Sunday from Mount Oliphant to Leglen Woods and explored every den and dell.

Mrs. Dunlop's maiden name was Wallace and she was a descendent of the patriot.

LITTLEHILL FARM   Map Ref. 467 305
Situated one mile north of the B744 Tarbolton/Galston Road, one mile east of Crosshands on the A76 Kilmarnock/Mauchline Road.

It is a neighbouring farm to Lochlea and, according to the poet's younger sister, Isabella Burns Begg, was the home of Isabella Steven, known locally as Tibbie Stein. She also said that Tibbie was the heroine of the song O'TIBBIE, I HAE SEEN THE DAY.

Tibbie also lived in Tarbolton while Burns was in the area. She inherited some money and thereafter rejected the poet's advances, giving rise to the song.
Also see: Bridge House; Tibbie Stein's House.

LITTLETON FARM   Map Ref. 217 073
Situated on the unclassified road from Kirkoswald to Girvan, one mile south-east of Turnberry.

The farm is thought to have been the home of Rab McGraen, who was referred to in the poem HALLOWE'EN — 'Our 'stibble-rig' was Rab McGraen.'

McGraen was related to the poet's mother, whose grandmothe~ was called Agnes McGraen. Her grandparents, John Broun and Agnes McGraen lived at Littleton before they moved to Craigenton Farm where they were joined later by the poet's grandparents, Gilbert Broun and Agnes Rennie.
Also see: Craigenton Farm.

LOANFOOT HOUSE   Map Ref. 415 380
The house is no longer extant. It was situated about 200 yards south of Irvine Road, Kilmarnock, at Loanfoot Avenue.

It was the home of Robert Muir, Wine Merchant, Kilmarnock, subject of the poem EPITAPH ON ROBERT MUIR. He subscribed for 72 copies of the Kilmarnock Edition of the poet's work and 40 of the first Edinburgh Edition.

Burns and Muir corresponded and in a letter dated 7 March, 1788, the poet expressed his religious beliefs. The poet's high opinion of Muir is expressed in a letter dated 13 December 1789 to Mrs Dunlop of Dunlop — "Muir, thy weaknesses were the aberration of human nature, but thy heart glowed with everything generous, manly and noble; and if ever emanation from the all-good being animated a human form, it was thine."

Overlooking Lochlea from the Poet's route to Tarbolton (1985)

LOCHLEA FARM   Map Ref. 455 301
Situated on the Largie Toll/Craigie Road, 1½ miles south of the A719 Ayr/ Galston Road. It was commonly spelled Lochlie at the time of Burns. Locally, it is still pronounced 'Lochli'.

It was the home of the Burnes family from 1777 to 1784, after they left Mount Oliphant Farm, Alloway and before they moved to Mossgiel Farm, Mauchline. The buildings have changed and the fields have been enclosed, but the poet would easily recognise the farm that caused the family so much worry.

The terms of the lease of Lochlea led to bitter litigation between William Burnes and his landlord, David McLure, and led to financial loss for the Burnes family.

On 13 February, 1784 the poet's father died at Lochlea aged 63 years, and his coffin was conveyed to Alloway for burial on poles slung between two horses in tandem. One of the horses belonged to the family friend, John Tennant of Glenconner Farm, Ochiltree. It is not recorded to whom the other horse belonged but we can presume it may have been the Burnes family.

The route by which the funeral left Lochlea is not known but it is generally accepted as having left by the west end of the steading and travelled by Millburn (Map Ref. 444 297), then south on to the 'C' class road which joins the Ayr/ Galston and Tarbolton/Largie Roads; it would then turn south-west towards Mosside Farm (Map Ref. 431 290) on a road which ran parallel to the existing road but on the south side of the plantation called The Long Wood; from Mosside the route would be by Redrae (Map Ref. 424 287) to the hamlet of Fail (Map Ref. 421 287); it would skirt the ruined Fail Monastery, ford the Water of Fail a short distance south of the existing bridge and join the Ayr/Galston Road. The route from Fail to Alloway is not known.

The poet's youngest sister, Isabella Burns Begg revealed a scene from the father's death bed. As he was approaching death, William Burnes said that there was one of the family for whose future conduct he was afraid. Robert approached his father's bed and asked, 'O, Father, is it me you mean?' His father said that it was and Robert turned away and looked out of the window with tears in his eyes. Burns expressed the opinion some years later that his father did not like him but his brother Gilbert thought that the father's dislike was only in the poet's imagination.

It was from Lochlea that Burns frequented Tarbolton, attending a dancing class, setting up and attending the debating society called the Bachelors' Club and joining the Freemasons.

It was also from Lochlea that he went to Irvine to learn flax dressing. With his brother, Gilbert, he had grown flax on a piece of land given to them by their father. After the flax was processed for them it was spun and woven into cloth to make clothes for the family and servants. The good quality of their flax is shown by a notice that appeared in the Glasgow Mercury newspaper under the title — Gainers of the Premium for Flax Raising Crop, 1781 and showed 'Mr. Robert Burns, Lochlie Farm, Tarbolton Parish — £3!' The poet went to Irvine to learn flax dressing so that the family would be able to do all of their own processing and possibly to give them another means of earning money.

An incident on the farm was recorded by the poet in the poem THE DEATH AND DYING WORDS OF POOR MAILIE. Gilbert told the story which inspired the composition. 'Robert', he said, 'had, partly by the way of frolic, bought a ewe and two lambs from a neighbour, and she was tethered in a field adjoining the house at Lochlea. He and I were going out with our teams, and our two younger brothers to drive for us, at midday, when Hugh Wilson (Hughoc of the poem), a curious-looking boy, clad in plaidings, came to us with much anxiety in his face, with the information that the ewe had entangled herself in the tether and was lying in the ditch. Robert was much tickled with the ewe's appearance and postures on the occasion. Poor Mailie was set to rights, and, when we were returned from the plough in the evening, he repeated to me the 'Death and Dying Words' pretty much in the way they now stand.'

Burns had started to write poetry at Mount Oliphant but it was at Lochlea that he developed from occasional rhymer to inspired poet.

Lochlea is worthy of a visit. Walk up to the top of the hill to the south-west of the steading and see the farm laid out below you. To your right you will see the depression which in the poet's time held the loch from which the farm took its name (when the loch was drained in the 19th century an ancient crannog/lake dwelling was revealed). From the depression, a burn still flows through the fields; imagine the brothers soaking and beating their flax in its waters. In your mind see the poet cutting up over the hill and passing you on his way to Tarbolton; or see Hughoc finding Poor Mailie and running to tell his masters. Try to visualise the death-bed scene in the steading or the funeral procession leaving the farm and passing down the valley towards Millburn on your left. 'From scenes like these' a greater understanding springs.

Also see: Bachelors' Club; Glasgow Vennel; Irvine; Shawwood; Tarbolton.

LOCHRIDGE ESTATE   Map Ref. 415 447
Situated on the A735 Kilmaurs/Stewarton Road, one mile south of Stewarton.

When the poet's uncle, Robert Burnes, moved to Ayrshire from the east of Scotland about 1748, he lived at Titwood Farm, near Stewarton.

Initially he worked at lime quarries at Lochridge but, later, he became crippled with rheumatism and moved to Stewarton.

Also see: Stewarton; Titwood Farm.

LOGAN HOUSE   Map Ref. 588 207
The house is no longer extant. It was situated on the south bank of the River Lugar, overlooking the west end of Lugar village. The site is indicated by

Logan Avenue, Cumnock which follows the line of the main driveway to the house. It can be seen that the mature trees lining Logan Avenue are considerably older than the modern houses.

Logan was the home of Hugh Logan, designated Laird of Logan, who was probably the subject of the mock epitaph starting — 'Here lies Squire Hugh'. The poem is normally published in The Merry Muses.

In a letter to James Dalrymple of Orangefield, dated February, 1787 Burns referred to Hugh Logan, 'Let the Worshipful Hugh Logan, or Mass James McKindlay, go into their primitive nothing'.

LOUDOUN ARMS & NEWMILNS CASTLE

LOUDOUN ARMS   Map Ref. 536 373
        Situated on the north side of Main Street, Newmilns, at its junction with Castle Street. The premises are still extant.

On 27 March, 1786, Burns was made an Honorary Member of Lodge Loudoun Kilwinning Newmilns No. 51 at a meeting held in a room in the Loudoun Arms. The minutes of the meeting record that 'much to the satisfaction of the Lodge', the poet was introduced by his friend and patron, Gavin Hamilton, Mauchline, then Right Worshipful Master.
Also see: Freemasonry; Newmilns.

LOUDOUN CASTLE   Map Ref. 506 377
        Situated east of the A719 Galston/Glasgow Road, one mile north of Galston.

It was the home of James Mure Campbell, 5th Earl of Loudoun. When the Earl and his wife, Flora McLeod of Raasay, died within a few weeks of each other in 1786, the Earl having committed suicide because of financial difficulties, Burns composed the poem *RAGING WINDS AROUND HER BLOWING.* The poem was dedicated to Flora's sister, Isabella McLeod of Raasay.

The castle was also the home of James Henri and his wife, Susan, second daughter of the poet's friend and patron, Mrs Dunlop of Dunlop. Mrs Henri gave birth to a son 4 months after the death of her husband and Burns made the birth the subject of the poem *ON THE BIRTH OF A POSTHUMOS CHILD.*

Mrs Dunlop lived at Loudoun Castle with Mrs Henri for a few months and Burns corresponded with her there.

Janet Little, a minor poetess known as 'The Scottish Milkmaid Poet', who corresponded with Burns and visited him at Ellisland, Dumfries worked at Loudoun Castle dairy. She is buried in the ancient Loudoun kirkyard near Loudoun Castle.

Also see: Dunlop House; Patie's Mill.

REV. DR. GEORGE LAWRIE

LOUDOUN KIRK   Map Ref. 537 373
Situated on the south side of Main Street, Newmilns.

The present church is not the original. It was re-erected on the site of the original in 1844.

The Rev. Dr. George Lawrie, friend and patron of Burns, was minister of Loudoun Kirk from 1763 to 1799. In 1786 he was impressed by the Kilmarnock Edition of the poet's work and brought it to the attention of Doctor Thomas Blacklock, a blind poet and influential literary figure in Edinburgh. As a result Burns delayed and later abandoned his plans to take up a post in the West Indies.

The poet became a friend of the Lawrie family and stayed with them at Loudoun Manse on more than one occasion. It is probable that he attended the original church with the family.

Rev. George Lawrie was succeeded in the kirk by his son, the Rev. Dr. Archibald Lawrie, also a friend of the poet. Father and son are both buried in the kirkyard.

The church should not be confused with the ancient ruin called Loudoun Kirk on the north bank of the River Irvine, a short distance west of Loudoun Castle, Galston. Janet Little, a minor poetess known as 'The Scottish Milkmaid Poet', who corresponded with Burns and visited him at Ellisland, Dumfries, is buried in the ancient kirkyard.

Also see: Loudoun Manse; Newmilns; St. Margaret's Hill.

LOUDOUN MANSE   Map Ref. 527 372
The manse of the poet's time is still occupied. It is now a private house called St. Margaret's Hill, at No. 116 Loudoun Road, Newmilns.

It was the manse occupied by the Rev. George Lawrie, minister of Loudoun Parish Kirk, Newmilns. Rev. Lawrie, an accomplished man, was impressed by the Kilmarnock Edition of the poet's work and sent a copy to Doctor Thomas Blacklock, Edinburgh, blind poet and influential literary figure in the capital. As a

LOUDOUN MANSE, 1985

result of Lawrie's intervention and Blacklock's acclaim, Burns delayed and later abandoned his plans to take up a post in the West Indies.

Burns was invited to the manse and became friendly with the Lawrie family. The poem *ON SENSIBILITY* or *RUSTICITY'S UNGAINLY FORM* was written to Mrs Mary Lawrie after the poet felt that the lady had given him a mild rebuke during a visit. It was enclosed in a book sent to one of the family.

On a visit by the poet during September, 1786 one of the daughters, Christina, played the spinet; it was the first time Burns had heard the instrument and he was enthralled. Rev. Lawrie and his wife led the company in dancing and the poet danced with the other daughter, Louisa. The refined but friendly atmosphere of the manse made a deep impression on Burns. Next morning he was late for breakfast and the son of the family was sent to enquire. He met Burns on the stair and asked if he had slept well. "Not well", said the poet, "the fact is, I have been praying half the night. If you go into my room, you will find my prayer on the table". The prayer was the poem *LINES WRITTEN AT A FRIEND'S HOUSE* or *PRAYER — O THOU DREAD POWER.*

The son of the manse was later the Rev. Dr. Archibald Lawrie. He succeeded his father at Newmilns and was also friendly with Burns.

The poem *THE NIGHT WAS STILL* relates to the night of the dancing in the manse and was given by the poet to Miss Louisa Lawrie who presented it later for publication.

The name St. Margaret's Hill was given to the house by the Rev. George Lawrie and it is referred to as such in some of the poet's correspondence. The house has been altered greatly since it was visited by Burns; wings were added, ceilings were heightened, attics were removed, and a bedroom used by Burns is now a passageway. The Rev. George Lawrie had the initials 'G.L.' and 'M.C.' carved in stone on the front wall of the house, and at a later date had the inscription 'Jehovah Jireh' added to it; 'G.L.' and 'M.C.' were George Lawrie and his wife, Mary Campbell. The initials and inscription are still extant.

Tradition maintains that on a window pane in the bedroom he occupied in the manse, Burns inscribed with a diamond — 'Lovely Mrs. Lawrie, she is all charms'. The window sash and pane were removed when the house was altered and are now preserved in the modern Loudoun Manse, Newmilns. Expert opinion considers the inscription to be genuine.

The Lawrie family are buried in Loudoun Kirkyard, Newmilns.

Also see: Loudoun Arms; Loudoun Kirk; Monkton; Newmilns; Patie's Mill; St. Margaret's Hill.

LUGAR RIVER
Map Ref. 493 252

The river joins the River Ayr from the south, between Haugh and Barskimming, one mile south of Mauchline at the Map Reference shown.

It is referred to in the poem THE BRIGS OF AYR — 'Or stately Lugar's mossy fountains boil' — and in the poem EPISTLE TO WILLIAM SIMPSON — 'While Irwin, Lugar, Ayr and Doon, Naebody sings'.

In the song MY NANIE, O', Burns originally composed the first line as 'Beyond yon hills where Stinchar flows' — and so it appeared in print until 1794. In a letter to George Thomson, song collector, in 1792, Burns wrote — 'the name of the river is horribly prosaic — I will alter it.' He then gave a choice of Girvan and Lugar. Thomson chose Lugar and so it has remained in many editions.

The date of the song and the identity of the heroine are in doubt and have caused much debate. The poet gave no clear inidcation.

Also see: Coldcothill Farm; Doura Farm; Girvan River; Kirkoswald; Minnybae Farm; Pinvalley; Ship Inn; Stinchar Rover.

MAIDENS VILLAGE

Situated on the Ayrshire coast, 15 miles south of Ayr.

Burns was familiar with that part of the coast now called Maidens. The village called Maidens did not appear on a map until about 1828. Previously, rocks in Maidenhead Bay had been called The Maidens of Turnberry.

The area at the centre of the present village was called Douglaston, still a familiar name, and the other parts of the area took their names from the dwellings — Ardlochan, Hogston, Jameston, Morriston, Shanter, etc.

The poet visited the area while staying at Ballochneil Farm between Maidens and Kirkoswald.

The places of interest in the area are dealt with separately.

Also see: Ardlochan; Damhouse of Ardlochan; Glenfoot; Hogston; Shanter Farm; The Cellars.

MANSON'S INN
Map Ref. 432 273

A Tarbolton inn at the time of Burns; it is no longer extant. It was situated on the east side of Burns Street, at its junction with Garden Street. The site is indicated by a plaque on a small pillar in the front garden of a house at the junction.

James Manson, the innkeeper, is referred to in the poem TO DOCTOR MACKENZIE — 'An' taste a swatch o' Manson's barrels.'

At a meeting of Lodge St. James Tarbolton in Manson's on 27 July, 1784, Burns was elected Depute Master. James Manson was treasurer of the Lodge.

The first man made a mason by Burns was Matthew Hall, an Ayr musician, well known throughout Ayrshire.

Manson is buried in Tarbolton kirkyard.

Also see: Freemasonry; Tarbolton.

MANSON'S INN, circa 1900

MARY MORISON'S HOUSE   Map Ref. 497 274 and 498 273
    Two locations in Mauchline are said to have been the site of Mary Morison's home. The first was in a house called 'Brownlea' which stood on the east side of Castle Street, at its junction with The Knowe. The other house was in a tenement building called 'The Place' which occupied all of the east side of the Cross, on the site now occupied by the Post Office.
    Mary Morison lived with her father, a retired army officer known locally as Adjutant Morison. They are both buried in Mauchline kirkyard.
    Mary died in 1791, aged 20 years. Her headstone, erected in 1825, records that she was the heroine of the song *MARY MORISON.* As she was only 15 or 16 years of age when the song was composed, it is now generally accepted that she was not the girl to whom the song was written. The heroine of the song is popularly thought to have been Alison (Ellison) Begbie, a servant at Carnell House between Mauchline and Kilmarnock who was courted by the poet while he was at Lochlea. This arises mainly from the poet's brother, Gilbert Burns having said that the song *MARY MORISON* was written to the same girl as the poem *BONIE PEGGY ALISON.* As the name Peggy Alison is accepted as being euphonious for Alison Begbie, on Gilbert's judgement the song *MARY MORISON* is also attributed to Alison Begbie.
    Although it can not be proved, tradition in Mauchline maintains that the poet showed friendly admiration for the young Mary Morison, daughter of Adjutant Morison, whom he met at tea in a friend's home. This tradition, and the wording on Mary's headstone, were supported by the Rev. Dr. Edgar, 19th Century minister of Mauchline Parish Church in his book Old Church Life In Scotland when he recorded — "I am informed, on authority, that a member of the Adjutant's family, who lived to be a grandmother, used to speak of Burns as one whom she knew personally, when he lived at Mauchline, and that she believed her sister Mary was the 'lovely Mary Morison' whom the poet admired."
    In a letter dated 20 March, 1793, to George Thomson, song collector,

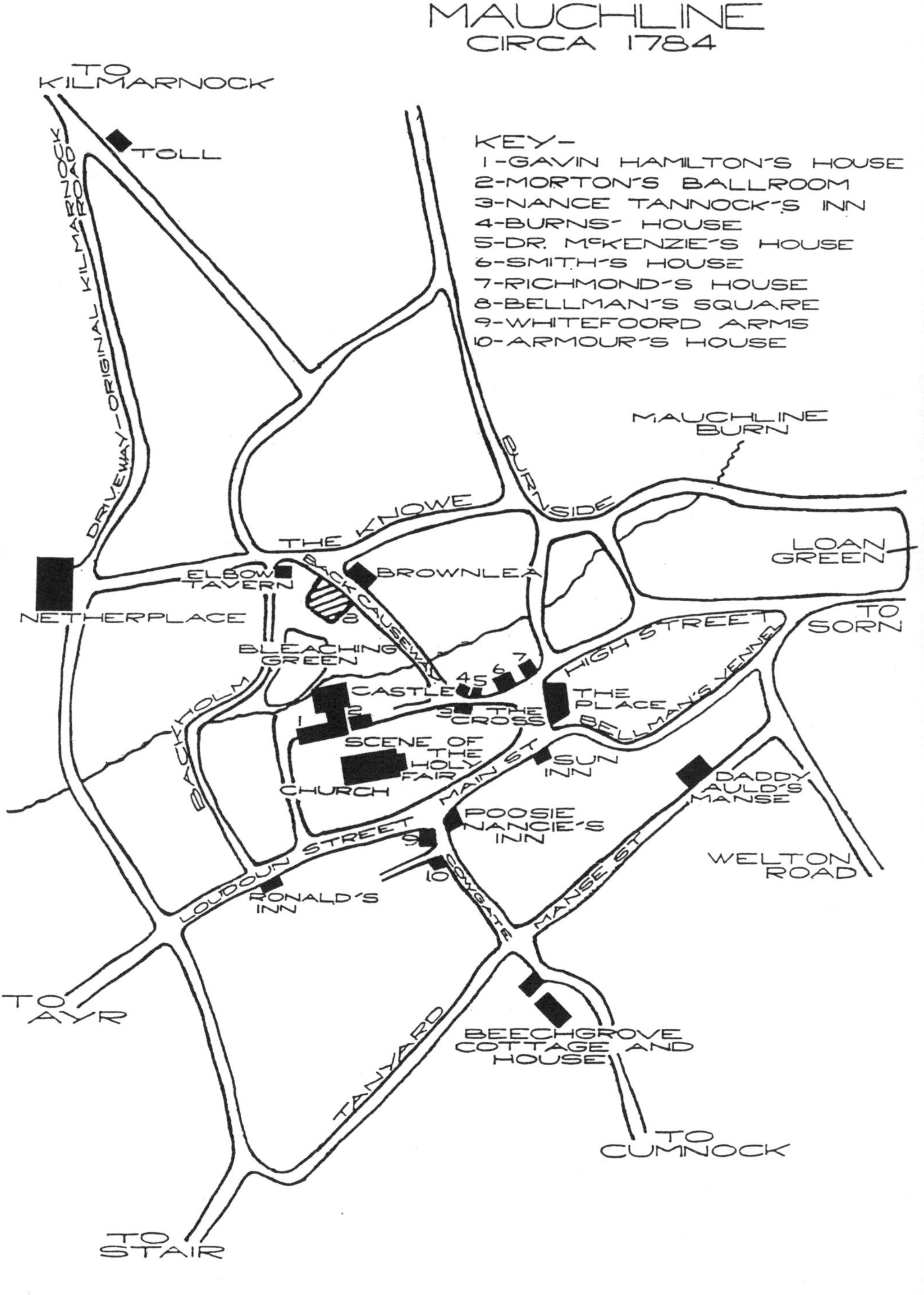

MAUCHLINE
CIRCA 1784

TO KILMARNOCK

TOLL

DRIVEWAY—ORIGINAL KILMARNOCK ROAD

KEY—
1-GAVIN HAMILTON'S HOUSE
2-MORTON'S BALLROOM
3-NANCE TANNOCK'S INN
4-BURNS' HOUSE
5-DR. McKENZIE'S HOUSE
6-SMITH'S HOUSE
7-RICHMOND'S HOUSE
8-BELLMAN'S SQUARE
9-WHITEFOORD ARMS
10-ARMOUR'S HOUSE

MAUCHLINE BURN

BURNSIDE

THE KNOWE

LOAN GREEN

ELBOW TAVERN

BROWNLEA

BACK CAUSEWAY

TO SORN

NETHERPLACE

HIGH STREET

BLEACHING GREEN

BACKHOLM

CASTLE

THE CROSS

BELLMAN'S VENNEL

THE PLACE

SCENE OF THE HOLY FAIR

CHURCH

MAIN ST.

SUN INN

DADDY AULD'S MANSE

LOUDOUN STREET

POOSIE NANCIE'S INN

MANSE ST.

WELTON ROAD

RONALD'S INN

COWGATE

TO AYR

TANYARD

BEECHGROVE COTTAGE AND HOUSE

TO CUMNOCK

TO STAIR

MAUCHLINE CROSS, circa 1900, with 'The Place' on the right

Back Causeway
circa 1900 with
Brownlea House
on the right.

Edinburgh, Burns wrote that the song *MARY MORISON* was 'one of my juvenile works'. If that is true, it is unlikely that either Mary Morison or Alison Begbie was the heroine of the song.

Mary Morison died as a result of the amputation of a foot seriously injured in an accident.

Also see: Back Causeway; Carnell House; Mauchline Kirkyard; Old Place.

MAUCHLINE
      Situated at the junction of the A76 Kilmarnock/Dumfries Road and the A758 Ayr/Muirkirk Road.
      The town is an important centre in the Burns Country. Although the poet lived at Mossgiel one mile north of the town, for only 4 years from March, 1784 to June, 1788, it was the period in which his poetic genius burst into full flower. In Mauchline he wrote in his finest medium, his native dialect, and on his best

subjects, the people around him. The Kilmarnock Edition of his poetry, his first time in print, was published on 31 July, 1786.

After he left Mauchline, Burns returned regularly to visit his mother, brother Gilbert, and other members of the family at Mossgiel.

The town and district have changed considerably but much of both would be easily recognised by the poet.

The street now called Castle Street was Back Causeway; Loudoun Street from The Cross to Cowgate was called Main Street; the main road through the town centre from north to south was by Back Causeway, The Cross, Main Street and Cowgate; the road through from east to west has not changed.

Earl Grey Street and Kilmarnock Road from The Cross to The Knowe were not created until about 1820. Examination of each side of Kilmarnock Road, just north of The Cross will show the gradient of the slope from the back gardens of High Street down to Castle Street. The amount of infilling required to level the ground shows why the main road ran by Castle Street and not straight through to The Cross as at present.

The young men in Mauchline with whom Burns became most intimate were James Smith, shopkeeper; John Richmond, clerk; William Hunter, shoemaker; and John 'Clockie' Brown, watchmaker. During June and July, 1786 he wrote to David Brice, a Mauchline shoemaker who had moved to Glasgow but nothing else is known of Brice or the friendship.

Local men older than the poet who showed him friendship and patronage were Gavin Hamilton, writer (lawyer); Doctor John Mackenzie, the family physician; Peter Morison, cabinetmaker; and John Dow or Dove, Innkeeper.

The many places of interest in the town and district are dealt with separately.

Also See: Armour's House; Back Causeway; Ballochmyle; Barskimming; Barskimming Mill; Beechgrove Cottage; Bridge Holm; Cowgate; Haugh; Mary Morison's House; Mauchline Bleaching Green; Mauchline Burn; Mauchline Castle; Mauchline Races and Fair; Mauchline Kirkyard; Mossgiel Farm; Nance Tannock's Inn; Netherplace; Poosie Nancie's Inn; Richmond's House; Smith's House; Whitefoord Arms.

MAUCHLINE BLEACHING GREEN   Map Ref. 498 272

The Green is no longer extant as such and is now only a rough piece of waste ground. It was situated to the west of Back Causeway (Castle Street) and north of the 'Castle'.

The poet's wife Jean Armour, was the daughter of James Armour, a master stone mason and contractor in Mauchline, and a man of some standing in the district.

Local tradition maintains that Burns and Jean Armour first spoke to each other on the bleaching green. The poet had attended a dance in the village on the evening of Mauchline Races in 1784. His collie dog had followed him to the village and into the dance and the poet remarked that he wished he could find a lass who would love him as faithfully as his dog. Jean was at the dance and overheard the remark.

A few days later, Jean was laying out clothes on the bleaching green when the poet went past on his way into the village. His dog ran amongst the clothes but returned to Burns when called to. Jean asked if he had yet found his faithful lass and he stopped and spoke to her.

From the meeting on the bleaching green sprang the romance of Robert Burns and Jean Armour, one of the classic romances of history.

The accuracy of the story concerning the meeting on the bleaching green was refuted by Jean many years later, but she may have done so because the story suggests that she made the first advance.

Also see: Armour's Home.

'A SEQUESTERED SPOT'
Mauchline Burn, where it joins the River Ayr at Stairaird

MAUCHLINE BURN   Map Ref. 473 257
The burn flows west through Mauchline to join the River Ayr at Stairaird, at the Map Reference shown, 2 miles west of Mauchline. Locally it is known as the River Chalk.
Whereas it is generally accepted that Burns and Highland Mary Campbell parted at Failford where the River Fail joins the River Ayr, as indicated by the monument on the north bank of the Fail, it has also been suggested that the parting was at Stairaird where the Mauchline Burn joins the River Ayr. A wood near Kingencleugh, Mauchline has also been suggested as the location of the parting.
The description of the parting given by Burns — 'We met by appointment, on the second Sunday of May, in a sequestered spot by the banks of Ayr' — can be applied to the Failford, Stairaird and Kingencleugh locations. However, in the opening stanza of the poem *HIGHLAND MARY*, the poet gave another indication of the spot — *'Ye banks and braes and streams around, The castle o' Montgomery!
. . . . For there I took the last Farewell, O' my sweet Highland Mary.'* This supports the claim of Failford as of the three it was the location nearest to Montgomerie House (Coilsfield).
Also see: Failford; Fail Water; Kingencleugh; Stairaird.

MAUCHLINE CASTLE   Map Ref. 497 274
Situated in Mauchline town centre, north of the kirkyard and west of Castle Street.
The 'castle' dates from the 12th Century and is thought to have been associated with Melrose Abbey, the monks of which had title to the land around Mauchline.
The ruined 'castle' was a prominent feature in Mauchline when the poet lived at Mossgiel Farm and frequented the village. His youngest sister, Isabella Burns Begg, when discussing Highland Mary Campbell, said that she knew little

about her but had overheard the poet telling their Mossgiel employee, John Blane, that 'Mary had refused to meet him in the old castle' and presumed later that he had been referring to Mary Campbell.

The poet's friend and patron, Gavin Hamilton, lived in the house adjacent to the 'castle' on its west side and his address was normally shown as Mauchline Castle. The house is still occupied.

Also see: Gavin Hamilton's House; Mossgiel Farm.

MAUCHLINE KIRK AND CASTLE before 1827

MAUCHLINE KIRKYARD   Map Ref. 497 273

Situated in Loudoun Street, Mauchline, 50 yards west of The Cross.

The present church was built in 1827 on the site of the original. The kirkyard was the setting of the poem THE HOLY FAIR.

A chart on the outside wall of the church indicates the burial places of the following list of the poet's family and associates:—

1. James Hamilton — See Mossgiel Farm.

2. Gavin Hamilton — See Gavin Hamilton's House.

3. Mary Morison — See Mary Morison's House.

4. Robert Wilson — Subject of the song THE GALLANT WEAVER. A native of Mauchline, he moved to Paisley for several years. When Jean Armour's parents found that she was pregnant by Burns, for the first time, they sent her off to relations in Paisley. An ill-founded rumour reached the poet that Jean and Robert Wilson were to be married and it caused him to be resentful of Jean.

5. William Fisher — See Montgarswood Farm and South Auchenbrain Farm.

6. Nance Tannock — See Nance Tannock's Inn.

7. James Bryan — Referred to by Burns as 'The Godly Bryan' in the poem THE COURT OF EQUITY and again in a letter to John Richmond dated 9 July, 1786. He was a

farmer at Welton Farm, one mile south-east of Mauchline. The Kirk session records show that he appeared in front of the session for 'irregularities' with girls.

8. George Gibson, his wife, 'Poosie Nancie' and daughter, 'Racer Jess'

See Poosie Nancie's Inn.

9. James Whitefoord

Infant son of Sir John Whitefoord of Ballochmyle. See Ballochmyle.

10. John Brown

Friend of Burns, referred to in the poem THE COURT OF EQUITY as 'Clockie Brown' because he was a watchmaker in Mauchline. The Brown family were well known makers of watches and clocks, especially of grandfather clocks.

11. John Richmond

See Richmond's House.

12. Rev. William Auld

See Symington.

13. Andrew Noble

School master at Mauchline and session clerk of the Parish kirk while Burns was at Mossgiel and appearing before the session for misdemeanours with Jean Armour.

14. James Humphrey

See Failford.

15. The Poet's children

Jean (twin of Robert, the eldest son), died September, 1786; un-named twins, died March, 1788; Elizabeth Riddell, died November, 1795.

16. 'Laird' McGavin

Referred to as 'Master Tootie, alias Laird McGaun' in the poem TO GAVIN HAMILTON, ESQ. He is thought to have been a rogue cattle dealer in Mauchline.

17. Burial place of the Alexanders of Ballochmyle.

Wilhemina Alexander, the 'Bonie Lass Of Ballochmyle' is NOT buried in Mauchline but at Inchinnan a disused cemetery within the bounds of Glasgow Airport.
See: Ballochmyle

MAUCHLINE RACES AND FAIR

Mauchline Races and Fair are referred to in the poem FIRST EPISTLE TO J. LAPRAIK — 'But Mauchline Race or Mauchline Fair, I should be proud to meet you there.'

At the time of Burns, Mauchline Races were held in the vicinity of the site of Burns Monument and Cottage Homes and were run from there past Mossgiel to Skeoch Hill and back.

Mauchline Fair was held at the Cross which was much the same as at present, except that Kilmarnock Road and Earl Grey Street had not been created and the houses extended from Castle Street (Back Causeway) across to High Street.

The Fair should not be confused with the religious celebration held in the kirkyard and immortalized by Burns in the poem THE HOLY FAIR.

MAULESIDE   Map Ref. 331 521

Situated on the A737 Dalry/Beith Road, one mile west of Beith.

William Ronald, one of the farm workers at Mossgiel referred to in the poem THE INVENTORY, was a farmer at Mauleside later in his life. At Mossgiel he acted as gauds boy (ploughman's assistant) when Burns was ploughing.

William Ronald's uncle, John Ronald, was the Mauchline/Glasgow carrier and probably the keeper of Ronald's Inn, Mauchline.
Also see: Mossgiel Farm; Ronald's Inn.

MAYBOLE

Situated on the A77 Ayr/Girvan Road, 10 miles south of Ayr.
The poet was familiar with the town and district.

Agnes Broun, the poet's mother, lived in Maybole for about 13 years. Her mother died when she was 10 years old, in 1742, and when her father re-married 2 years later, Agnes went to live with her maternal grandmother, Mrs. Rennie, in Maybole. When her grandmother died, she moved to the home of her paternal uncle, Willie Broun, also in Maybole. The locations of the houses are not known.

The poet's parents, William Burnes and Agnes Broun, met at Maybole Fair in 1756. A bust of the poet looks down on the High Street from the apex of the gable at No. 15 and, according to local tradition, marks the site of the booth where William and Agnes met at the Fair.

The poet's friend and correspondent, William Niven (cousin of John Niven of Ballochneil), was the son of a Maybole farmer and shopkeeper and lived in the town. They met as fellow-pupils at Hugh Rodger's school, Kirkoswald in 1775. While attending the school, Burns lodged at Ballochneil Farm, south of the village but he spent weekends at William Niven's home at Maybole.

William Niven became a wealthy and avaricious businessman. He served on Maybole Town Council and was a Depute Lord Lieutenant of Ayrshire. He built himself a house in High Street, the site of which is now occupied by the Bank of Scotland at No. 67. He bought Kirkbride Farm and inherited Kirklandhill Farm from his father.

In September, 1786, the poet visited Maybole to collect subscription money for the Kilmarnock Edition of his poems. He lodged at the Kings Arms Hotel which was situated in High Street, immediately south of the District Council offices at No. 70, until it was destroyed by fire a few years ago. The poet was joined for the evening by a group of his friends, including William Niven; Hugh Rodger, his old schoolmaster; David Dunn, Maybole schoolmaster; and Thomas Piper, assistant to Doctor Hugh Logan, Maybole's only physician.

After a convivial night, some of his friends gathered next morning to say goodbye to him. Burns had hired a horse from the Kings Arms for his journey home; it was a mare called Rosinante, well known throughout the area as a broken-down nag. As was the custom, his friends went ahead of him and awaited his arrival on what is now the Maybole/Alloway High Road, a half mile out of the town. As he approached them they gave him a reception of salutes and mock heroic verses, to which the poet said, "Why all this parade of fine verses, my friends, it would have been enough to say — Here comes Burns on Rosinante, She's damned poor, but he's damned cantie".

When he returned to Mossgiel the poet wrote to William Niven in a letter dated 20 August, 1786 and sent his regards to his Maybole friends.
Also see: Ballochneil Farm; Kirkoswald.

MAYFIELD

In a letter dated 22 August, 1792, to Mrs. Dunlop of Dunlop, Burns wrote that he had been visited at Ellisland Farm, Dumfries by Mr. Baillie of Mayfield and his daughters.

Mr Baillie's daughter, Lesley, was the heroine of the songs *SAW YE BONIE LESLEY* and *BLYTHE HAE I BEEN ON YON HILL*.

The Baillie family lived at Mayville, Stevenston and it must be presumed that Burns called it Mayfield by mistake. In later correspondence to Lesley Baillie, he referred to her home as Mayville.

The name Mayfield has another Burns association. Bruce Campbell, with whom Burns corresponded in a letter dated 13 November, 1788, was designated as being of Mayfield, Milrig and Sornbeg. These properties were in Galston Parish and had no connection with the Baillie family.
Also see: Mayville House; Milrig House.

MAYVILLE HOUSE, 1985

MAYVILLE HOUSE   Map Ref. 268 422
Situated at No. 31 High Road, Stevenston, the house is still occupied.
It was the home of Lesley Baillie, heroine of the songs *SAW YE BONIE LESLEY* and *BLYTHE HAE I BEEN ON YON HILL*. Born at Mayville on 6 March, 1768, she married Robert Cumming of Logie and died at Edinburgh on 12 July, 1843.
Robert Baillie of Mayville erected a memorial column to his wife; Lesley's name was added to it later. It now stands on the east side of Glencairn Street, Stevenston, alongside No. 110. Originally it was erected much nearer Kerelaw Mains. It became derelict and lay in pieces for many years until restored and re-erected on its present site in 1929.
Legend in Stevenston maintains that Burns visited the Baillie family at Mayville. He did visit them but probably while they were living in a town house in Edinburgh.
The Baillie family visited Burns at Ellisland Farm, Dumfries during August, 1792, when they were en route to England. After the visit, the poet accompanied them on horseback for the first few miles towards the border. To compliment Lesley Baillie and commemorate the visit, Burns composed the song *SAW YE BONIE LESLEY* — '*O' saw ye bonie Lesley, As she gaed o'er the border.*'

During May, 1793, Burns wrote a letter to Lesley Baillie at Mayville.

According to Lesley Baillie's daughter, Lesley assisted Burns with the immortal last verse of his poem *LAMENT FOR JAMES, EARL OF GLENCAIRN*. It is claimed that originally the last two lines were — *'I'll remember gude Glencairn, And a' that he has done for me'*. On the poem being read to the Earl's sisters, the word 'gude' was objected to and the word 'great' suggested instead. Burns felt that 'great' was inappropriate but did not wish to offend the family. On a visit to the Baillie family he mentioned his dilemma to Lesley. She suggested omitting both 'gude' and 'great' and making the lines — *'I'll remember thee, Glencairn, and a' that thou hast done for me'*. Burns was delighted by the suggestion and adopted the lines for publication of the poem. The story can not be verified but it has a ring of truth.

MILNCRAIG HOUSE   Map Ref. 399 208

Situated north of the A70 Ayr/Cumnock Road, one mile west of Coylton.

It was the home of Sir William Augustus Cunninghame who was referred to as *'The Bauld Sir Willie'* in the poem *THE AUTHOR'S EARNEST CRY AND PRAYER*.

MILRIG HOUSE   Map Ref. 502 341

Situated east of the B744 Galston/Crosshands Road, 2 miles south of Galston.

The original house was demolished shortly after World War II. It was the home of Bruce Campbell, designated as of Mayfield, Milrig and Sornbeg. Burns corresponded with Campbell in a letter dated 13 November, 1788 and sent him subscription sheets for the Kilmarnock Edition of his poems. There is no other record of association between the men.

Also see: Mayfield.

MILTON   Map Ref. 436 236

Situated on the B730 Tarbolton/Drongan Road, at Stair Bridge. It is the correct name of the hamlet on the north bank of the River Ayr, commonly regarded as Stair.

Burns was familiar with the area and visited the nearby Stair House with David Sillar, who was courting Peggy Orr, nurserymaid to Mrs Stewart of Stair.

In his book Burns and Stair (1927), John McVie records that Mary (Mailly) Crosbie, housekeeper to Mrs Stewart, who had joined Peggy Orr in entertaining Burns and Sillar in the kitchen of Stair House, lived and died in a cottage at Milton. Local tradition maintains that Burns took tea in the cottage.

Mailly Crosbie's cottage is no longer extant and its exact location is unknown. It is thought to have been sited on the east side of the Tarbolton/Drongan Road, about 100 yards north of Stair Bridge.

Also see: Stair; Stair House.

MINNYBAE FARM   Map Ref. 234 068

Situated on the east side of the A77 Kirkoswald/Girvan Road, a half mile south of Kirkoswald.

It was the home of William Neilson who married Peggy Thomson of Kirkoswald in 1784. Peggy was the heroine of the composition *SONG — COMPOSED IN AUGUST*. The poet's sister, Mrs Begg, said that the song *MY NANIE, O'* was written to Peggy Thomson but other girls are also suggested as the heroine of this song.

Burns visited the Neilsons, presumably at Minnybae, in 1786 shortly before he was due to leave for the West Indies. He gave Peggy a signed copy of the Kilmarnock Edition of his poems with the poem *LINES TO AN OLD*

SWEETHEART inscribed on the flyleaf. The poet later recorded that William Neilson walked with him for the first 3 miles of his journey home.
Also see: Coldcothill Farm; Doura Farm; Girvan River; Kirkoswald; Peggy Thomson's House; Pinvalley; Ship Inn; Stinchar River.

REV. DR. THOMAS BURNS

MONKTON
     Situated one mile north of Prestwick and a half mile west of the A77 Kilmarnock/Ayr Road.
     The Rev. Andrew Mitchell, minister of Monkton Parish Church from 1775 to 1811, was referred to in the poem *THE KIRK'S ALARM* as '*Andrew Gowk*'. He is buried in Monkton kirkyard.
     The poet's nephew, the Rev. Dr. Thomas Burns, was minister at Monkton from 1830 to 1847. He was the son of the poet's brother, Gilbert Burns, and was born at Mossgiel in 1796. His daughter, Ann Burns, great-niece of the poet, died at Monkton and is buried in the kirkyard. A plaque on the outside wall of the present Monkton Church, Monkton Road, Prestwick shows that it was — 'built 1837 by Rev. Thomas Burns, Minister from 1830 to the dissolution in 1843. In 1848 he led a party of Free Church emigrants to New Zealand and there founded the provinces of Otago and Southland.'
     Another Monkton Minister was the Rev. George Lawrie who was the incumbent from 1844 to 1878. He was the son and grandson of the poet's friends the Rev's. Archibald and George Lawrie of Newmilns and was born in Loudoun Manse. While at Monkton, Rev. Lawrie published a book of poems, the best known being the still popular song *HA'E YE MIND O' LANG, LANG SYNE*. He died on 14 February, 1878 and is buried in Monkton kirkyard.
     Monkton kirkyard has another important association with Burns. A headstone commemorates Matthew Paterson and his wife Ann Ronald, of

Aikenbrae Farm, Monkton. Matthew Paterson was an associate of Burns in Tarbolton and a member of the Bachelors' Club. Ann Ronald was one of the *Ronalds of the Bennals* and referred to in the poem of that name. The poet had been keen to court Ann but was afraid of being rebuffed because of her family's superior social standing.
Also see: Aikenbrae Farm; Bennals Farm; Loudoun Kirk; Patie's Mill.

MONTGARSWOOD FARM   Map Ref. 530 277
Situated on the south side of the B743 Mauchline/Sorn Road, 2 miles east of Mauchline.

William Fisher, farmer and kirk elder, has been described as having lived at Montgarswood Farm. There are now two Montgarswood Farms and Fisher lived at the farm now called East Montgarswood.

Fisher was immortalised by Burns as *Holy Willie* of the poems *HOLY WILLIE'S PRAYER* and *HOLY WILLIE'S EPITAPH*. He is also referred to in the poem *THE KIRK'S ALARM*.

In the 18th Century the Mauchline/Sorn Road ran on the south side of the farm, not on the north as at present. The site of Fisher's dwelling was to the west of the modern steading and at the west side of the site now occupied by Sorn Mine.

William Fisher was found dead in a snow-filled ditch on South Auchenbrain Farm Road during February, 1809. He is buried in Mauchline kirkyard.

Montgarswood has another association with Burns. In the 18th century it was purchased by a Mauchline merchant, Henry Richmond, father of the poet's close friend, John Richmond. John Richmond's brother, James, took over the property in 1798.
Also see: Mauchline Kirkyard; Richmond's House; South Auchenbrain Farm.

MONTGOMERIE HOUSE   Map Ref. 446 263
The house is no longer extant; only its driveways remain. It was situated north of the A758 Ayr/Mauchline Road, one mile east of the B730 Tarbolton/ Stair Road.

Between 1806 and 1809. Coilsfield House, home of the Montgomerie family, was demolished and a new mansion built on or near the site. The new residence was called Montgomerie House.

Burns was almost certainly familiar with the estate. Mary Campbell, the poet's Highland Mary, is thought to have worked at Coilsfield as a dairy maid. In the song *HIGHLAND MARY*, Burns referred to Coilsfield as 'the Castle o' Montgomerie' and this has led to some confusion in differentiating between the earlier Coilsfield and later Montgomerie Houses.
Also see: Coilsfield House.

MONUMENTS, MEMORIALS AND STATUES

1.   Alloway — Burns Monument and Gardens.
     Situated on the north bank of the River Doon, at the north end of Old Doon Bridge. The monument, designed by Thomas Hamilton, was opened on 4 July, 1823. The three-sided base represents the three divisions of Ayrshire — Carrick, Cunninghame and Kyle.
     The interior of the monument contains important Burns relics, including Jean Armour's wedding ring, the bible Burns gave to Highland Mary Campbell, and the poet's seal.
     The imaginative statues of Tam O'Shanter, Souter Johnie and Nance Tannock by James Thom the self-taught Ayrshire sculptor, are located in the beautiful gardens surrounding the monument.
     The monument and gardens are open to the public from April to September for a small admission charge.

BURNS MONUMENT, ALLOWAY

BURNS MONUMENT, KILMARNOCK

THE NATIONAL BURNS MEMORIAL,
MAUCHLINE

2. Ayr — Burns Statue.
    Situated in Burns Statue Square, Ayr, the statue by G.A. Lawson, FRSA,
    was unveiled on 11 July, 1891.

3. Failford — Memorial to Burns and Highland Mary.
    Situated on the west bank of the Fail Water at Failford on the A758 Ayr/
    Mauchline Road, 2½ miles west of Mauchline.
    The memorial commemorates the parting of Burns and Highland Mary
    Campbell. It was unveiled on 14 May, 1921.
    Also see: Failford.

4. Irvine — Burns Statue.
    Situated on Irvine Moor, overlooking the east bank of the River Irvine, 150
    yards south of Maress Road. The statue, by Pittendrigh MacGillivray, was
    unveiled on 18th July, 1896.

5. Kilmarnock — Burns Monument and Statue.
    Situated in Kay Park, Kilmarnock, a few hundred yards north-east of the
    town centre, the monument was opened on 9 August, 1879. It incorporates
    a museum of minor items and is open to the public by prior arrangement
    with the curator. The statue was sculpted by W.G. Stevenson.

6. Mauchline — National Burns Memorial and Cottage Homes.
    Situated at the junction of Kilmarnock Road and Skeoch Road, Mauchline,
    the memorial and cottage homes neighbour the fields of Mossgiel Farm. The
    memorial, opened on 7 May, 1898, incorporates a museum of minor relics
    and interesting items, and gives a panoramic view of the Burns country. The
    cottage homes are maintained for elderly persons by charitable Burns
    organisations.

MORTON'S BALLROOM
    The ballroom was in Mauchline but the exact location is unkown. It was
described by a contemporary of Burns as the house nearest to Mauchline Castle on
the east side. It was probably on the south-west corner of a square of houses on
the site now occupied by the Parish Church Hall.
    Hugh Morton, the proprietor, has been described as an innkeeper and the
ballroom was probably a hall or large room in the inn.
    Tradition maintains that Burns and Jean Armour met at a dancing class in
the ballroom. The poet's dog had followed him to the dance and he remarked that
he wished he could meet a lass who would love him as faithfully as his dog did. A
few days later Jean was on Mauchline bleaching green when the poet passed and
she asked him if he had met his faithful lass yet. So started their romance.
    One traditional version of the marriage of Burns and Jean Armour maintains
that it was performed in Hugh Morton's ballroom by John Farquhar-Gray, J.P. of
Gilmilnscroft, Sorn. There is no official record of the place of marriage.
Also see: Gavin Hamilton's House; Gilmilnscroft; Mauchline Bleaching Green;
Ronald's Inn.

MOSSGIEL FARM   Map Ref. 489 286
    Situated on the 'C' class Mauchline/Tarbolton Road, one mile north of
Mauchline Cross. Burns normally spelled the name Mossgiel but also used the
old spelling, Mossgavill.
    Burns lived at Mossgiel for 4 years, from 1784 to 1788, part of which time
he spent in Edinburgh and on his tours of Scotland. It is doubtful if any man in
literature has ever made a name so famous by such a brief assocation. The
Frenchman, Auguste Angellier in his 'Etude sur la vie et les oeuvres de Robert
Burns' (1893), wrote (in translation), — 'Mossgiel, Mossgiel, how that name sings
itself into every Scottish heart.' Mossgiel — a modest, unpretentious farm that has

given its name to a multitude of streets, houses and clubs throughout the world.

Originally there were three Mossgiels neighbouring each other — East, West and South. East Mossgiel is still a working farm. South Mossgiel can only be detected as stones in a clump of trees, 50 yards from the Mauchline/Tarbolton Road opposite the driveway to West Mossgiel.

Burns lived at West Mossgiel. It is now a prosperous and productive farm. The dwelling-house still exists but it has been subject to extensive alteration. In 1858 the house was re-modelled and in 1870 a new storey and roof were added. The buildings may have changed and the fields been enclosed but the poet would still be at home on the farm.

It was during his stay at Mossgiel that the poet's genius burst into full flower and his work was published for the first time. The finest work of the period includes the following:— *THE VISION; ADDRESS TO THE UNCO GUID; THE EPISTLES TO DAVIE; THE EPISTLES TO J. LAPRAIK; HALLOWE'EN; THE JOLLY BEGGARS; THE COTTER'S SATURDAY NIGHT; THE ORDINATION; THE HOLY FAIR; THE AUTHOR'S EARNEST CRY AND PRAYER; ADDRESS TO THE DEIL; SCOTCH DRINK; HOLY WILLIE'S PRAYER AND EPITAPH; THE LASS O' BALLOCHMYLE; THE TWA DOGS; THE BRIGS OF AYR; TO A MOUSE; TO A MOUNTAIN DAISY; DEATH AND DOCTOR HORNBOOK;* and many more. A torrent of genius.

The '*daisy*' field where the '*tender stem*' was crushed '*amang the stoure*', and from which a mass of daisies have gone with visitors to colonise the corners of the earth, is immediately behind the steading. The '*mousie*' field where the poet ploughed up '*that wee bit heap o' leaves an' stibble*' is north-east of the steading, bordered on its east side by the Mauchline/Kilmarnock Road. A large field, two fields removed from the back of the steading, is known as Knockhaspie's Land, and is possibly the origin of the name Knockhaspie's Land in the song *HIGHLAND HARRY BACK AGAIN.*

Stand at Mossgiel at daybreak and see '*the rising sun o'er Blacksideen*' (*A MAUCHLINE WEDDING*), or, '*upon a simmer morn — snuff the caller air*' and see '*the rising sun, owre Galston muirs*' (*THE HOLY FAIR*) and you know that you are in the Land of Burns. Imagine the cotter wending his weary way homewards from the back fields of Mossgiel as '*November chill blaws loud wi' angry sugh*' (*THE COTTER'S SATURDAY NIGHT*) and you will enjoy the poem even more when next you read it. See the sun setting behind Arran and you will wonder as many have done, how this great poet made no poetic acknowledgement of such magnificence. Only once did Burns make even an oblique reference to the sunset behind Arran; in a letter dated 18 November, 1786 to Miss Wilhelmina Alexander, enclosing the song addressed to her, *THE LASS OF BALLOCHMYLE*, he described the setting which inspired the poem — '*I had roved out . . . to view nature in all the gaiety of the vernal years. The sun was flaming over the distant western hills.*' From Mauchline, the reference can only be to Arran.

We know more about the workers employed at Mossgiel than at any other of the Burns family farms.

ROBERT ALLAN — the poet's half-cousin, son of the Allans of Fairlie and Old Rome, was employed as a ploughman.

WILLIAM RONALD — nephew of John Ronald the Mauchline carrier was also employed as a ploughman. Later in life he farmed on his own behalf at Mauleside, Beith. He spoke of the excellent way in which the poet conducted evening worship at Mossgiel.

DAVID HUTCHESON — '*wee Davoc*' of the poem *THE INVENTORY* worked as herd boy. His father had been a ploughman at Lochlea but died of fever, leaving 2 boys and 2 girls orphaned. The poet took David and his sister Janet into his household. He took a special interest in the boy and looked after him until he was able to make his own way in the world. Janet worked for the poet's mother for many years.

MOSSGIEL, circa 1850

JOHN BLANE — he worked as a gauds boy (ploughman's assistant). Many years later when he was coachman on the Cumnock/Kilmarnock coach, he was interviewed by James Grierson, Burns researcher, and claimed to have been in church with Burns when the incident occurred which inspired the poem *TO A LOUSE*. He also told of having been chastised by Burns for flicking a whip at a sparrow and removing some of its feathers. He said that the poet's manner made such an impression on him that he could never have done such a thing again.

JOHN LAMBIE — he was also employed as a gauds boy. He claimed to have been leading the plough for Burns when the poet turned over the nest of the field mouse. He had gone running after the mouse 'wi murdering pattle' until Burns stopped him. The poet had gone quiet for some time after the incident and laters showed Lambie the draft of the poem *TO A MOUSE*, saying, 'Well, what do you think of your mouse now?'

JAMES HAMILTON — as a very young boy he worked at the farm and acted as the poet's messenger boy. He recalled having been sent to Mauchline with a note for Jean Armour, with the instruction to give it to no one but her. He died in Mauchline in 1862, aged 84 years, and is buried in the kirkyard.

WILLIAM PATRICK — he worked for the poet as a labourer. As an old man he lived in Loudoun Street, Mauchline and was interviewed regularly by researchers. His reminiscences about Burns and his Mauchline associates can be read in the book Robert Burns at Mossgiel by William Joly (1881). He died in Mauchline in 1864, aged 88 years, and is buried in the kirkyard.

Also see: Galston; Knockhaspie's Land; Mauchline; Mauchline Castle; Mauchline Kirkyard; Mauleside; Old Rome; Stevenston.

MOUNT OLIPHANT FARM

MOUNT OLIPHANT FARM   Map Ref. 357 173

Situated a half mile south of Corton Road, and a half mile east of the A77 Ayr/Maybole Road.

The Burnes family moved from the cottage at Alloway to Mount Oliphant at Whitsun, 1766 when the poet's father, William Burnes rented the farm from Doctor William Ferguson of Doonholm, Alloway, Provost of Ayr. At the time of the move, the poet was 7 years of age.

When 14 years of age and still at Mount Oliphant, Burns composed his first song, *HANDSOME NELL*, to a young girl called Nellie Kilpatrick of Purclewan Mill whom he met while they were working together in a harvest field.

The farm proved to be infertile and the Burnes family were close to poverty. As the eldest of the family, the poet had to labour in the fields in all weathers, adversely affecting his health for the rest of his life. In an autobiographical letter written many years later, the poet called the farm 'A ruinous bargain'.

It was from Mount Oliphant that Burns attended schools at Ayr, Dalrymple and Kirkoswald.

In 1777, the family moved on to Lochlea Farm, Tarbolton Parish. In all they had lived at Mount Oliphant for 11 years, considerably longer than the poet lived at any other place.

The farm buildings have changed, the fields have been enclosed and neighbouring properties have changed greatly, but the poet would still find the area reasonably familiar.

If you visit Mount Oliphant, stand and look around you. This land saw the formative years of Robert Burns. Here he *'padl'd in the burn'* and *'pou'd the gowans fine' (AULD LANG SYNE)*, from here he explored the wooded *'banks and braes o' bonie Doon'* and it was here that he dreamt his first dreams of young love. This land may have shown the Burnes family the misery of poverty and drudgery but it nurtured the God-given genius of an embryo poet.

Also see: Ayr; Dalrymple; Kirkoswald; Purclewan.

MUIRKIRK
Situated on the A70 Ayr/Edinburgh Road, 10 miles east of Cumnock.
The poet was familiar with the area by passing through en route between Mossgiel Farm and Edinburgh and by his visits to the Rhymer, John Lapraik.

Lapraik lived at Dalfram, Muirsmill, Netherwood and Nether Wellwood, all a few miles to the west of Muirkirk, and finally moved into the village. In Muirkirk, he ran an ale-house which was also the post office; it was situated in Kirkgreen, on a site later occupied by the old catholic school. He is buried in the kirkyard.

Burns referred to Muirkirk and Lapraik in the poem *(FIRST) EPISTLE TO J. LAPRAIK* — *'They tauld me 'twas an odd kind chiel, about Muirkirk.'*

The Rev. John Shepherd, referred to as *'Muirland Jock'* in the poem *THE KIRK'S ALARM*, was Minister of Muirkirk Parish Church from 1775, probably to his death in 1799, but this can not be confirmed.
Also see: Dalfram; Muirshill.

MUIRSMILL   Map Ref. 658 263
The house is no longer extant. The site is on the north bank of the River Ayr, almost opposite Nether Wellwood, on the A70 Muirkirk/Cumnock Road, 3 miles west of Muirkirk.

For a short period it was the home of John Lapraik, minor poet, who was an acquaintance of Burns. He was the subject of the three *EPISTLE(S) TO J. LAPRAIK*.

Burns visited Lapraik at least once and stayed overnight at Muirsmill.
Also see: Dalfram; Muirkirk.

John Murdoch's house in which Burns lodged.

MURDOCH'S HOUSE   Map Ref. 335 219
A stone plaque on the south gable of the premises at No. 58, Sandgate, Ayr, indicates the site of John Murdoch's house.

In 1765, when he was 18 years of age, Murdoch was interviewed by the poet's father, William Burnes, in Simpson's Inn, Ayr and appointed to teach the children of Burnes and some of his neighbours, at Alloway. Murdoch was required to produce a specimen of his handwriting for examination.

The school at Alloway was held in a tenement building described as being near Burns Cottage, which was demolished in 1878.

Although the Burnes family moved 2 miles from Alloway to Mount Oliphant Farm in 1766, Robert and Gilbert continued to attend the Alloway School until about 1768. Murdoch became friendly with the Burnes family and visited them regularly.

John Murdoch left the area for a few years but returned in 1773 when he was appointed English Master at Ayr Grammar School. Shortly after his appointment, Robert Burnes attended the Grammar School for 3 weeks to improve his English and French. While at the school he lodged with Murdoch in his home in Sandgate.

In 1776, Murdoch left Ayr under a cloud; while intoxicated he had spoken out indiscreetly against the Rev. Dr. William Dalrymple, minister of Ayr Auld Kirk.

He went to London where he met the poet's brother, William Burnes. When William died he assisted with the funeral arrangements. From London, he spent some time in Paris where he met and was befriended by Colonel Fullarton of Fullarton, Troon. Colonel Fullarton later befriended and corresponded with Burns. John Murdoch died in London and was buried in St. Andrew's Gardens burial ground, Greys Inn Road, on 20 April, 1824.

Also see: Alloway; Ayr Grammar School; Fullarton House; Simpson's Inn.

MUSEUMS, DISPLAYS ETC.

1. Alloway — Burns Cottage and Museum
    Situated on the west side of the B7024 Ayr/Maybole Road, in Alloway Village, 2 miles south of Ayr town centre.
    Burns Cottage, the poet's birthplace, was restored and opened to the public in March, 1901. The museum has one of the world's finest collections of Burns relics; it is open from 9.00 a.m. to 7.00 p.m. daily throughout the year.
    Also see: Burns Cottage; New Gardens.

2. Alloway — The Land o' Burns Centre
    Situated on the east side of the B7024 Ayr/Maybole Road, 200 yards north of the River Doon and 2½ miles south of Ayr town centre.
    The centre was opened on 21 June, 1977. It incorporates an audio-visual display on the life of Burns, a book and gift shop, and a beautiful garden with a picnic area and static display of old farm machinery. It is open from 9.00 a.m. to 6.00 p.m. daily throughout the year.
    The centre is an ideal starting point for a tour of the Burns Country.

3. Alloway — Burns Monument
    Situated on the east side of the B7024 Ayr/Maybole Road, at the north end of Old Doon Bridge, 2½ miles south of Ayr town centre.
    The interior of the monument is a small museum containing important Burns relics, including Jean Armour's wedding ring, the bible Burns gave to Highland Mary Campbell, and the poet's seal.
    It is open to the public from 9.00 a.m. to 7.00 p.m. daily from April to October.
    Also see: Monuments, Memorials and Statues.

4.   Ayr — Tam O'Shanter Museum
     Situated on the east side of High Street, at Nos. 230/232.
     The museum contains a few minor items of interest.
     The building is an excellent example of an 18th Century dwelling house and
     shows the type of house that was in High Street when Burns was in Ayr.
     There is no evidence to suggest that it was frequented by Burns or Douglas
     Graham, the poet's model for Tam O'Shanter; neither is there evidence to
     support it as the scene of the market day carousel of Tam and Souter Johnie
     with the landlord and wife described in the poem TAM O'SHANTER.
     The history of the house can be read in the beautifully produced booklet
     The Dwelling House of James Shearer by Joseph D. Shearer (1983).
     The museum is open to the public from 9.00 a.m. to 7.00 p.m. daily from
     April to October.

5.   Irvine — Glasgow Vennel
     Situated on the east side of Townhead, about 300 yards south of The Cross.
     The workshop in which Burns learned flax heckling and the house in which
     he is said to have lodged have been restored.
     The heckling shop has an audio-visual display on the poet's association with
     Irvine and a collection of flax dressing equipment. It is connected to
     another restored house which contains a shop and an exhibition room. The
     heckling workshop, exhibition room and shop are open to the public from
     10.00 a.m. to 4.00 p.m. daily except Sunday, throughout the year.
     The lodging house has been furnished in the style of the 18th century. It is
     also open to the public from 10.00 a.m. to 4.00 p.m. daily except Sunday,
     throughout the year.
     Also see: Glasgow Vennel.

6.   Irvine — Irvine Burns Club Museum
     Situated at "Wellwood', No. 28 Eglinton Street.
     An excellent museum with a valuable collection of Burns manuscripts
     including Wilson the printer's copies of the poems THE HOLY FAIR and
     THE COTTER'S SATURDAY NIGHT. In the friendly, intimate atmosphere
     the average visitor is likely to get closer to a Kilmarnock Edition or a
     manuscript than in any other museum.
     It is open to the public from 2.00 p.m. to 5.00 p.m. on Sundays throughout
     the year or at almost any reasonable time by prior arrangement with the
     Club Secretary who can be contacted at the Club's telephone number.

7.   Kilmarnock — Burns Monument
     Situated in Kay Park, a few hundred yards north-east of the town centre.
     The monument incorporates a museum of minor items. It is open to the
     public by prior arrangement with the Curator, Dick Institute, London Road,
     Kilmarnock.
     Also see: Monuments, etc.

8.   Kilmarnock — Burns Federation Headquarters
     Situated in the Dick Institute, London Road, Kilmarnock, a few hundred
     yards east of the town centre.
     The world-wide Burns Federation was instituted in Kilmarnock in 1885
     with the motto 'A Man's A Man For A' That.' The Burns Chronicle has been
     published annually since 1892.
     The objectives of the Federation are:—

     1)   To strengthen and consolidate by universal affiliation the bond of
          fellowhship existing amongst the members of Burns Clubs and kindred
          societies.

2) To purchase and preserve manuscripts and other relics connected with the poet.

3) To repair, renew, or mark with suitable inscriptions, any building, tombstones, etc., interesting from their association with Burns.

4) To encourage and arrange school competitions in order to stimulate the teaching of Scottish history and literature.

An excellent collection of important Burns relics and manuscripts can be viewed by prior arrangement with the Curator.

9. Kirkoswald — Souter Johnie's Cottage
Situated on the east side of the A77 Maybole/Girvan Road in Main Street, Kirkoswald.
John Davidson, prototype of the character *Souter Johnie* in the poem *TAM O'SHANTER* lived in the cottage from 1785 to his death in 1806.
The cottage contains a collection of minor items and a display of souter's (shoemaker's) tools. Imaginative statues of Tam O'Shanter, Souter Johnie, the landlord and his wife, all from the poem *TAM O'SHANTER*, and sculpted by self-taught Ayrshire sculptor, James Thom, are displayed in a building in the back garden of the cottage.
The cottage is open daily from April to September.
Also see: Souter Johnie's Cottage.

10. Largs — Burns Garden
Situated at the east end of Douglas Park Garden, Irvine Road.
The garden is planted with the flowers referred to in the poems and songs of Burns.

11. Mauchline — Burns House Museum
Situated in Castle Street, a few yards from The Cross.
The house in which Burns and Jean Armour started married life and the adjoining house which was owned by the poet's friend, Doctor John Mackenzie, are maintained as a museum and contain several Burns relics and items of interest. It is open daily throughout the year.
Also see: Back Causeway.

12. Mauchline — The National Burns Memorial
Situated at the junction of Kilmarnock Road and Skeoch Road.
The memorial incorporates a museum of minor relics and interesting items. It is open to the public by arrangement with the curator of the Burns House Museum, Mauchline.
Also see: Monuments, etc.

13. Mauchline — Poosie Nancie's Inn
Situated in Loudoun Street, at its junction with Cowgate.
The inn was the setting of the cantata, Love And Liberty, better known as The Jolly Beggars. It contains a museum of minor relics and interesting items and is open to the public daily throughout the year.
Also see: Poosie Nancie's Inn.

14. Tarbolton — The Bachelors' Club
Situated in Sandgate, a few yards from The Cross.
The premises in which Burns, his brother Gilbert, and 5 other young men founded the debating society called the Bachelors' Club. It was also the building in which the poet was initiated into Freemasonry.
It is furnished in the style of the 19th Century and contains several items of interest, including the Tyler's Sword of Lodge St. David Tarbolton and a toddy bowl and jug which belonged to Peggy Orr, a servant at Stair House and friend of Burns.
It is open to the public daily throughout the year.
Also see: Bachelors' Club.

15.   Tarbolton — Lodge St. James
      The temple of Lodge St. James is situated at No. 65 Montgomerie Street, It
      was inaugurated in 1925.
      Burns was a member of the Lodge from 1782 and Depute Master from 1784
      to 1788. The Lodge possesses several valuable relics and interesting items
      connected with the poet's membership, including minute books entered and
      signed by the poet and his brother, Gilbert, a letter sent by Burns to the
      Lodge on 23 August, 1787, and the mallet, apron and chair used by the
      poet.
      On 9 August, 1844 the poet's 3 surviving sons visited the Lodge and were
      made honorary members. Their signatures are amongst the items held by the
      Lodge.
      The relics can be viewed by prior arrangement with the Lodge.
      Also see: Freemasonry.

NANCE TANNOCK'S INN   Map Ref. 497 274
      Situated in Castle Street (Back Causeway), Mauchline, a few yards out of
The Cross. It was built about 1712 and is still extant but not as an inn.
      The correct name of the establishment was The Sma' Inn. Nance Tannock —
also spelled Tinnock or Tunnock — was the maiden name of Mrs Agnes Weir who
ran the inn.
      The inn had the distinction of giving direct access to Mauchline kirkyard
from its rear door. It was the place referred to as the 'change-house' in the poem
THE HOLY FAIR — 'Now but and ben the change-house fills.'
      Burns also referred to the inn in the poem THE AUTHOR'S EARNEST
CRY AND PRAYER — 'An drink his health in auld Nance Tinnock's.'
      In the Glenriddell Manuscript, Burns noted that the poem TO MR.
MCADAM OF CRAIGENGILLAN was composed extempore in Nance Tannock's
Inn, Mauchline, on receipt of a note from that gentleman.
      Nance Tannock said that Burns had been in her inn only once or twice.
Also see: Sma' Inn.

NETHERPLACE   Map Ref. 428 371
      Netherplace House was demolished shortly after the Second World War. It
was situated west of the A76 Mauchline/Kilmarnock Road, and north of the A758
Mauchline/Ayr Road, on the western edge of Mauchline.
      It was the home of William Campbell, who was the subject of the poems
EPITAPH ON A HENPECKED SQUIRE, EPIGRAM ON SAID OCCASION and
'ANOTHER' — 'But Queen Netherplace of a different complexion.'
      The ancient name of the property was Cowfieldshaw or Cowfauldshaw.
      At one time the road out of Mauchline to Kilmarnock ran past the front
door of the house but later this road was restricted to use as the private driveway.

NETHERTON
      A district of Kilmarnock, still known by that name, situated on the B7038
Kilmarnock/Ayr Road, a half mile south of the town centre.
      In the 18th Century it was an area, then on the outskirts of Kilmarnock,
frequented by weavers. It was referred to in the poem THE ORDINATION — 'Or
to the Netherton repair, An' turn a carpet weaver'.
      Kilmarnock weavers produced many rhymers, foremost amongst them being
Gavin Turnbull who lived in poverty in Soulis Street in the town centre. Turnbull
was acquainted with Burns and addressed a poem to him called THE BARD. He
took up acting and Burns met him again when he appeared at the Theatre Royal,
Dumfries. In 1793, Burns sent three of Turnbull's songs to George Thomson, song
collector, for consideration for inclusion in his collection of Scottish songs. Gavin
Turnbull died in America.
Also see: Kilmarnock.

NEWARK   Map Ref. 324 174
    The castle and estate are situated on the west side of the B7024 Alloway/
Maybole Road, a few hundred yards south of the River Doon.
    Nellie Kilpatrick, the heroine of the song *HANDSOME NELL*, the first
recorded composition by Burns, married William Bone, coachman to the Laird of
Newark and resided on the estate.
Also see: Purclewan.

NEW CUMNOCK
    Situated on the A76 Cumnock/Dumfries Road, 6 miles south of Cumnock.
    Burns was very familiar with the village and surrounding district from his
journeys between Mauchline and Ellisland. He had many friends in the district and
stayed regularly in a local inn. Legend maintains that he wrote the song *SWEET
AFTON* in the inn.
    The inn cannot be traced. Local tradition maintains that the existing Castle
Hotel was the inn concerned but this can not be substantiated. About 1900, the
inn in which Burns had lodged was described as then being a farmhouse on the
banks of the River Afton and that does not support the tradition concerning the
Castle Hotel which has no history of being a farmhouse.
    The Rev. James Young, *'Jamie Goose'* of the poem *THE KIRK'S ALARM*
was minister of New Cumnock Parish Church from 1758 to 1795. The original
church is now a ruin and Rev. Young is buried in the old kirkyard.
Also see: Afton River; Ashmark; Corsincon; Knockshinnoch; Laight; Pencloe.

NEW GARDENS   Map Ref. 335 186
    Situated on the B7024 Alloway/Maybole Road, in Alloway Village, 2½
miles south of Ayr town centre.
    The proprety now known as Burns Cottage was called New Gardens by the
poet's father, William Burnes, when he built it in 1757.
    William Burnes fued 7½ acres of land in Alloway from Dr. Alexander
Campbell of Ayr and built the cottage with his own hands. He called it New
Gardens as he intended to start a nursery. On 15 December, 1757, he married
Agnes Broun and started married life in the cottage.
    The poet was born there on 25 January, 1759.
Also see: Burns Cottage.

NEWMILNS
    Situated on the A71 Kilmarnock/Edinburgh Road, 7 miles east of
Kilmarnock, and astride the River Irvine.
    Burns was familiar with the area, mainly through his friendship with the
Rev. Dr. George Lawrie, minister of Loudoun Kirk, Newmilns and by his visits to
the manse.
    The poet was also acquainted with John Arnot, Dalwhatswood, Newmilns
and was an Honorary Member of Newmilns Masonic Lodge.
Also see: Dalwhatswood; Freemasonry; Loudoun Arms; Loudoun Kirk; Loudoun
Manse; Newmilns Castle; Patie's Mill.

NEWMILNS CASTLE   Map Ref. 536 373
    Situated in Castle Street, Newmilns, a few yards north of its junction with
Main Street.
    The castle or keep was originally a residence of the Campbells of Loudoun.
    It is referred to in the poem *THE NIGHT WAS STILL* — *'The night was
still, and o'er the hill, The moon shone on the castle wa'.'* The poet was staying
overnight with the Rev. Dr. George Lawrie and his family at Loudoun Manse and
saw the moon on Newmilns Castle from his bedroom window.
Also see: Loudoun Arms, Loudoun Kirk, Loudoun Manse; Newmilns.

OCHILTREE

Situated on the A70 Ayr/Cumnock Road, 4 miles west of Cumnock.

Burns was familiar with the village and district and had several friends in the area, namely, the Tennant family at Glenconner Farm, Auchenbay Farm and Ochiltree Mill, George Reid at Barquharrie Farm, and William Simson the local schoolmaster.

The village was referred to in the poem *EPISTLE TO WILLIAM SIMSON —* '*Or frosts on hills of Ochiltree, Are hoary grey*'. Simson was friend, correspondent and fellow rhymer to Burns. He was later schoolmaster at Cumnock where he died and is buried in the old cemetery.

The Rev. David Grant, '*Davie Bluster*' of the poem *THE KIRK'S ALARM*, was minister of Ochiltree Parish Church from 1786 to his death in 1791, aged 41 years; he is buried in the kirkyard. In a letter to Lady Elizabeth Cunninghame, the poet called Rev. Grant 'A designing, rotten-hearted Puritan.' John Tennant of Glenconner told Burns that his opinion of the minister was wrong. He introduced them and they became firm friends.

The poet's Kilmarnock friend, Tam Samson, who was referred to in the poems *TAM SAMSON'S ELEGY* and *EPITAPH*, was born in Ochiltree. His father was a market gardener opposite the Parish Church. His brother, John Samson, is buried in the kirkyard. In 1786. When Burns borrowed a horse from George Reid of Barquharrie Farm for his journey to Edinburgh, John Samson borrowed the horse from Burns for a journey back to Ayrshire.

John Tennant of Glenconner's eldest son, James Tennant, was miller at Ochiltree Mill. He was addressed by the poet in the poem *EPISTLE TO JAMES TENNANT OF GLENCONNER — 'Auld comrade dear and brither sinner.'*

Burns sent the poem to James Tennant by the hand of one, John Simson — *I've sent you here by Johnie Simson'*. Tradition maintains that Simson — no relation to William Simson the Schoolmaster — was an Ochiltree music and dancing teacher. In the poem, Burns exhorts Tennant to — '*Assist poor Simson a' ye can, Ye'll fin' him just an honest man.*' The Tennant family did assist Simson with the result that Ochiltree had its biggest ever dancing class.
Also see: Auchenbay Farm; Ayr Grammar School; Barquharrie Farm; Glenconner Farm; Poole; Tam Samson's House.

OLD DOON BRIDGE

OLD DOON BRIDGE   Map Ref. 333 178

Situated 200 yards upstream from the modern bridge carrying the B7024 Alloway/Maybole Road; it is generally called the Brig o' Doon.

Although not open to vehicular traffic, the bridge is maintained in good repair and is open to pedestrians. The age of the bridge is uncertain but it was built not later than the 15th Century and possibly as early as the 13th Century.

The bridge is featured in the poem *TAM O'SHANTER* as that over which *'Tam'* was pursued by the witches and where his horse *'Meg'* gained the safety of the key-stone *'but left behind her ain grey tail.'* By its association with the poem, the bridge must be one of the most famous pieces of architecture in the world.
Also see: Kirk Alloway; Tam O'Shanter's Journey.

OLD PLACE   Map Ref. 466 342
The property is no longer extant. It was situated south of the road leading to Cessnock Mill, Crossroads, about 200 yards west of the A76 Kilmarnock/Mauchline Road and 200 yards north of the A719 Ayr/Galston Road.
The house was an ancient home of the Campbells of Cessnock; when they built a new house near Galston, Old Place became a farmhouse. When eventually it was demolished, the land was incorporated into neighbouring farms and the site of the house is now on Shawsmill Farm.
According to John Muir, FSA (Scot.) in his booklet Burns At Galston And Ecclefechan (1896), Old Place was the home of the poet's early love, Alison (Ellison) Begbie.
In 1781, when Burns was 22 years of age and living at Lochlea Farm, he courted Alison Begbie who was then working at Carnell House which is on the River Cessnock, mid-way between Old Place and Lochlea. He wrote five romantic letters to her and she is thought to have been the heroine of the songs *THE LASS OF CESSNOCK BANKS* and *BONIE PEGGY ALISON (AND I'LL LOVE THEE YET).*
Burns proposed marriage to Alison but was rejected. In his autobiographical letter to Doctor John Moore in 1787, he wrote of the incident — "A belle fille whom I adored, and who had pledged her soul to meet me in the fields of matrimony, jilted me, with peculiar circumstances of mortification."
It is often said that the song *MARY MORISON* was written to Alison Begbie. This probably arose from the poet's brother, Gilbert Burns, having suggested that *MARY MORISON* was written to the same girl as the song *BONIE PEGGY ALISON.* It is easy to accept the euphonius name Peggy Alison for Alison Begbie but not so the name Mary Morison.
Also see: Carnell House; Mary Morison's House.

OLD ROME   Map Ref. 392 361
The area is indicated by Old Rome Farm on the Earlston Road, at its junction with the A759 Kilmarnock/Troon Road, at Gatehead.
As late as the early years of this century, a map of the district showed a row of cottages called Old Rome on the east side of the Kilmarnock/Troon Road, at the south end of the bridge over the River Irvine. The area has been known as Rome, Old Rome and Rumford and in the past has had a school and a distillery.
It has been erroneously claimed that the adjacent Fairlie Estate was originally called Old Rome or Old Rome Forest. There is nothing to support this claim as the estate was called 'Dreghorn' until it was bought by the Fairlies prior to 1689 and re-named.
In 1786, Jean Armour's father, James Armour, took out a warrant against Burns, hoping to obtain money to maintain Jean and the twins she was expecting by the poet. Burns went into hiding and while doing so he wrote to his Mauchline friend, John Richmond. The letter was dated 30 July, 1786 and addressed as from 'Old Rome Foord'. The location of the ancient ford can still be traced, a short distance upstream from the modern bridge over the River Irvine at Gatehead.
The address shows that Burns was living with his mother's half-sister Jean Broun and her husband, James Allan, a carpenter on Fairlie Estate. The couple had been married in 1775 and lived in a cottage on the estate, probably near Old Rome. Their son Robert Allan worked as a ploughman at Mossgiel. James died in 1789 and Jean moved into one of the houses in Old Rome cottages. She re-

married an Adam Baird of Dundonald and died in 1821, aged 71 years.

Fairlie Estate has another important connection with the Burnes family. When the poet's father, William Burnes, moved to Ayrshire from the east of Scotland in 1750, he took up employment as a gardener at Fairlie for about 2 years before he moved to Alloway.

In the Dundonald area, tradition maintains that William Burnes first met the poet's mother, Agnes Broun while she was visiting her half-sister, Mrs Allan. In fact, whereas William Burnes was at Fairlie between 1750 and 1752, Mrs Allan was not born until 1750. She was 18 years younger than the poet's mother and only 7 years of age when his parents were married.

Also see: Craigenton Farm; Fairlie House.

ORANGEFIELD HOUSE   Map Ref. 358 268
The house is no longer extant. Originally called Monkton House, it was situated east of the A79 Prestwick/Monkton Road, within Prestwick Airport, on the south side of the main runway. Until the new airport terminal was constructed, Orangefield was part of the terminal complex.

It was the home of James Dalrymple, patron and friend of Burns on the poet's early visits to Edinburgh. Dalrymple was cousin to two of the poet's other patrons, James Cunningham, 14th Earl of Glencairn and Robert Aiken, lawyer, Ayr. The Rev. Dr. William Dalrymple who baptised Burns, was James Dalrymple's uncle.

In a letter dated 13 December, 1786 to John Ballantine, lawyer, Ayr the poet referred to his first visit to Edinburgh and wrote — 'I have found a worthy, warm friend in Mr. Dalrymple of Orangefield, who introduced me to Lord Glencairn . . . '.

Although there is no record of Burns having visited Orangefield, he may have done so. In a suppressed stanza of the poem THE VISION, he described accurately the location of the house — 'The owner of a pleasant spot, near sandy hills' and in a note indicated that it referred to Dalrymple and Orangefield.

Unfortunately, James Dalrymple was extravagant and dissolute and squandered his fortune. In 1791 he was declared bankrupt and amongst the trustees appointed to oversee the dispostion of his property were the Rev. Dalrymple, Robert Aiken and John Ballantine. He died in Edinburgh in 1795.

Also see: Ayr Auld Kirk; Castlehill House; Whitehill.

PARK FARM   Map Ref. 223 063
Situated 200 yards east of the A77 Ayr/Girvan Road, 2 miles south of Kirkoswald.

In 1775, when Burns attended Rodger's School, Kirkoswald, and lodged at Ballochneil Farm, a fellow-pupil called Thomas Orr lived on Park Farm, neighbouring Ballochneil. The present Park Farm was then called Laigh Park. The property then called Park was probably also Laigh Park or the neighbouring property now called High Park.

Thomas Orr was the son of William Orr, farm worker, and his wife Jean Robinson. They lived in a cottage on Park and probably shared it with Jean's mother, Julia Robinson. Julia was reputed to be a witch, a reputation she probably cultivated to cover her association with smugglers.

The poet and Thomas continued their friendship after they met at school and corresponded with each other. In 1780, Thomas visited Lochlea and helped with the harvest.

In a letter dated 3 August, 1781, the poet's father, William Burnes, wrote to Thomas Orr from Lochlea — "Thomas — I want you to be here to your harvest by Monday first, for we begin on Tuesday (sic) to our wheat. My wife desires enquire, and bring her word how her brother John's wife is, — I am, yours, etc." Thomas answered the call and when he returned home he took messages from the poet to several Kirkoswald friends, including Peggy Thomson.

When Thomas was at Rodger's school he was studying navigation. He eventually went to sea in 1785 and was drowned on his first voyage.
Also see: Kirkoswald; Laigh Park.

PARK HOUSE   Map Ref. 339 209
The house is not extant. It was situated east of Carrick Road, Ayr, near what is now the junction of Bowman Road and Ballantine Drive. In the 18th Century it was outwith the town.
It was the home of the unmarried Major William Logan and his sister, Miss Susan Logan, with both of whom Burns corresponded. Major Logan was addressed in the poem *EPISTLE TO MAJOR LOGAN* — '*Hail thairm-inspirin, rattlin Willie.*' Susan was addressed in the poem *TO MISS LOGAN*, which the poet sent to her with the gift of a book of poems at New Year, 1787.
The poem to Major Logan ends with a reference to the house — '*sir Bard will do himself the pleasure, To call at Park.*'
Major Logan was a fiddler of some repute and regarded as a wit and a 'character'. The following anecdote is told about him — he had been unwell and was visited by his minister who said that he would have to suffer his ailment with fortitude, to which Logan replied, "Fortitude! Aye, Minister, it would take fiftytude."

PATIE'S MILL   Map Ref. 532 370
The mill is no longer extant. It was situated on the south bank of the River Irvine. The site is at the west end of Brown Street, Newmilns, on the north side, and is now occupied by a factory car park.
In the 18th Century rival locations in Ayrshire and Aberdeenshire were claimed as the subject of Allan Ramsay's Scottish Song The Lass O'Patie's Mill.
In a letter to George Thomson, song collector, dated 7 April 1793, Burns referred to the song and wrote — 'The following anecdote which I had from Sir William Cunningham of Robertland, who had it from the late John, Earl of Lowdon — Allan Ramsay was residing at Lowdon Castle with the then Earl, father of Earl John, and one afternoon, riding or walking out together, His Lordship and Allan passed a sweet romantic spot on Irvine water, still called 'Patie's Mill', where a bonnie lass was "tedding hay, bareheaded on the green". My Lord observed to Allan that it would be a fine theme for a song. — Ramsay took the hint; he composed the first sketch of it, which he produced at dinner.'
Burns must have been familiar with the location of Patie's Mill as it would be prominently seen from Loudoun Manse where he visited.
The mill had another very tenuous connection with the poet. It is referred to in the song *HA'E YE MIND O' LANG, LANG SYNE* by the Rev. George Lawrie of Monkton, son and grandson of the poet's friends Rev. Archibald and George Lawrie of Newmilns.
Also see: Loudoun Manse; Monkton; Newmilns.

PEGGY THOMSON'S HOUSE   Map Ref. 239 075
Situated in Main Street, Kirkoswald, and now part of the Shanter Hotel. Hugh Rodger's School, attended by Burns for one term in 1775, occupied what is now the south end of the hotel and Thomson's house occupied what is now the centre part of the premises.
One day in August, 1775, Burns went into the back garden of the school to take the altitude of the sun for his studies and saw Peggy in the back garden of her home.
In an autobiographal letter to Doctor Moore, dated 2 August 1787, Burns described his encounter with Peggy — 'A charming fillette, who lived next door to the school, overset my trigonometry, and set me off at a tangent from the sphere

of my studies . . . stepping out to the garden one charming noon to take the sun's altitude, I met with my angel.'

Thus, Peggy became the second girl to set the poet's pulse racing and as with the first, Nellie Kilpatrick, he was inspired to poetry. He composed the song *HAR'STE — A FRAGMENT* which he later expanded and renamed *SONG — COMPOSED IN AUGUST.*

In 1784, Peggy married William Neilson, Minnybae Farm, Kirkoswald. In 1786, shortly before his intended departure for the West Indies, Burns visited Peggy and William. He gave Peggy a signed copy of his newly published Kilmarnock Edition, in the flyleaf of which he inscribed the poem *LINES TO AN OLD SWEETHEART*. When he left them, William accompanied him on the first 3 miles of his journey before they took their sad farewells of each other.

The poet's youngest sister, Isabella Burns Begg, said that the song *MY NANIE, O'* was written to Peggy Thomson but there are other girls suggested as the heroine of the song.

Also see: Coldcothill Farm; Doura Farm; Girvan River; Kirkoswald; Pinvalley; Rodger's School; Ship Inn; Stinchar River.

PENCLOE   Map Ref. 618 095
Situated in Glen Afton, New Cumnock, one mile south of the town.

It was the home of Thomas Campbell to whom Burns wrote a letter dated 19 August, 1786, and addressed from 'Mr. J. Merry's, New Cumnock.'. The letter was a farewell message from Burns to Campbell on the poet's imminent departure for Jamaica. There is no other reference to Campbell and no record of any other association with the poet.

Burns had several friends in Glen Afton and it is generally thought that the friendships were established when the poet was journeying between Mauchline and Ellisland, Dumfries. As the poet paid his first visit to Ellisland in February, 1788 and took it over in May, 1788 the date and address on the letter to Campbell show that he had visited New Cumnock before he was concerned with Ellisland.

Also see: Afton River; Ashmark; Laight; New Cumnock.

PINVALLEY   Map Ref. 331 951
Situated about 3 miles east of Barr, and north of the Nick of the Balloch, on the Crosshill/Newton Stewart Hill Road.

The poet's aunt, Mrs Brown of Kirkoswald, wife of his maternal uncle, Samuel Brown of Ballochneil Farm, said that Burns wrote the song *MY NANIE, O'* to a girl called Agnes McIlwraith of Pinvalley.

According to his aunt, Burns met Agnes McIlwraith at Kirkdamdie Fair. The Fair, also called Kirkdominie Fair, was the largest feeing fair in south Ayrshire and was very ancient in origin. It was held annually on the last Saturday in May in the grounds of the ruined Kirk Domine which stands on the north bank of the River Stinchar, 1½ miles south-west of Barr.

In all editions of his work up to and including 1794, Burns made the first line of the song *MY NANIE, O'* — *'Behind yon hill where Stinchar flows.'* In a letter dated 26 October, 1792 to George Thomson, song collector, the poet wrote of the song — "The name of the river is horribly prosaic, I will alter it." He then gave a choice of Girvan and Lugar and observed — "Girvan is the river that suits the idea of the stanza best."

As Stinchar was the original choice and, of the others, Girvan suited the idea best, it is easy to conclude that the song was set in south Ayrshire. If the poet composed the song at Mount Oliphant or Kirkoswald, the setting sun would first darken the east, roughly where the upper reaches of the Stinchar and Girvan Rivers flow *'Mang moors an' mosses many, O'*, as in the first verse of the song. If south Ayrshire was the location, the otherwise unknown Agnes McIlwraith could have been the heroine.

It is generally accepted that the heroine was Agnes Fleming of Coldcothill or Doura Farms, neighbouring Lochlea. If she was, it is incredible that the poet chose Stinchar or Girvan as suitable rivers for his introduction, as neither of them bears any relationship to the sun setting in the west or first darkening the east as seen from Lochlea.

The poet's brother, Gilbert Burns, said that the heroine was Agnes Fleming; his youngest sister, Isabella Burns Begg, said that it was Peggy Thomson of Kirkoswald; in Girvan, local tradition maintains that it was Agnes Brown, daughter of the proprietor of the Ship Inn, Girvan; and Rev. Hamilton Paul, a 19th Century Burns scholar said that it was an Agnes Sheriff of Kilmarnock.

The poet gave no indication of the identity of the heroine. In his first Commonplace Book he commented — 'Whether the following song will stand the test, I will not pretend to say, because it is my own: only I can say it was, at the time, real.'

Also see: Coldcothill Farm; Doura Farm; Girvan River; Kirkoswald; Lugar River; Minnybae Farm; Ship Inn; Stinchar River.

POOLE   Map Ref. 497 212
Situated 200 yards north of Watston Farm, Ochiltree, which is a quarter mile west of the village and to the north of the A70 Ayr/Cumnock Road.

The home of Thomas Walker, tailor, was in the vicinity but its exact location is unknown. Walker was addressed in the poem *REPLY TO A TRIMMING EPISTLE RECEIVED FROM A TAILOR*. Walker was a friend of William Simson, schoolmaster, Ochiltree, subject of the *EPISTLE TO WILLIAM SIMSON*. He composed verses and sent them to Burns who did not reply. He then wrote to the poet and attacked his morals, prompting the poet to compose his 'Reply'.

Walker later gained some fame for a widely distributed religious pamphlet, A Picture Of The World. He died at Sorn Bridgend in 1833, aged 82 years, and is buried in Sorn Kirkyard.

Also see: Ochiltree.

POOSIE NANCIE'S INN   Map Ref. 498 274
Situated in Loudoun Street, Mauchline, at its junction with Cowgate. It is open to the public as a public house and museum. It was the setting of the cantata *LOVE AND LIBERTY*, better known as *THE JOLLY BEGGARS* — 'Ae night at e'en a merry core, O' randie, gangrel bodies, In Poosie-Nancie's held the splore, To drink their orra duddies.'

When Burns was in Mauchline, the landlord was George Gibson referred to as '*Black-bearded Geordie*' in the poem *ADAM ARMOUR'S PRAYER*. The name by which the inn was known is now unknown. Poosie-Nancie was the name given by the poet to Gibson's wife, Agnes Ronald. Their daughter Janet Gibson was referred to as '*Racer Jess*' in the poem *THE HOLY FAIR* — '*There Racer Jess and twa-three whores, Are blinkin at the entry*'; the name 'Racer' was derived from her fleetness of foot and her habit of running errands for payment and races for wagers. Their son Jock was referred to as '*Haveril*' (half-witted) Jock in the same poem.

An entry in Mauchline kirk session minutes for 1773 records that Agnes Ronald was habitually drunk and troublesome to her neighbours. She was summoned to appear before the Session and did so, only to tell them that she was determined to continue in her disorderly ways.

A later entry in the same year records that George Gibson kept a disorderly house and that his wife and daughter were guilty of resetting stolen goods.

Agnes Wilson, servant to George Gibson, was referred to as '*Geordie's Jurr*' *in the poem* ADAM ARMOUR'S PRAYER and was probably the '*Tozie Drab*' of the poem *LOVE AND LIBERTY*. An entry in the kirk session minutes refers to her as being 'of lewd and immoral practices and the occasion of the late

POOSIE NANCIE'S INN, circa 1890

disturbance.' The disturbance was probably the incident which Burns made the subject of the poem *ADAM ARMOUR'S PRAYER*. Jean Armour's brother, Adam, and a number of other young men subjected Agnes Wilson to the custom of 'riding the stang'; — for her prostitution and probably for spreading disease, they tied her astride a rough pole and carried her through the village.

Poosie Nancie should not be confused with Nance Tannock, keeper of the Sma' Inn, Mauchline.

Burns did not frequent Poosie Nancie's.

Also see: Mauchline Kirkyard; Museums, etc; Nance Tannock's Inn.

PURCLEWAN   Map Ref. 379 158

Situated between the A713 Ayr/Dalmellington Road and the B742 Dalrymple/Coylton Road, a half mile south of their junction.

When the Burnes family lived at Mount Oliphant Farm, Purclewan was a hamlet with a mill and a smiddy, less than 2 miles away. It was the home of Nellie Kilpatrick, heroine of the poet's first published song, *HANDSOME NELL*. Her father was the miller at Purclewan. Burns and Nellie met while working together in a harvest field in 1773, at which time Burns was 14 and Nellie 12 or 13 years of age. Nellie sang a song composed by a local laird's son and Burns tried to impress her by composing words to her favourite tune. Several years later, he wrote of the incident — 'thus with me began Love and Poesy.'

Nellie Kilpatrick married William Bone, coachman to the Laird of Newark and lived at Newark Estate. She died about 1820.

The blacksmith at Purclewan was Henry McCandlish. He lent the youthful Burns a copy of the book The Life of Wallace which fired him with a patriotic fervour that lasted all of his life.

The blacksmith's son, James McCandlish — he later dropped the 'Mc' — was the poet's lifelong friend. He studied medicine at Glasgow University and settled firstly in Edinburgh and later in Mauchline. He married Jean Smith of Mauchline, sister of the poet's friend James Smith, referred to in the poem *THE BELLES OF MAUCHLINE* — *'Miss Smith she has wit.'* Burns corresponded with Candlish. In a letter dated March, 1791 to Peter Hill, he described Candlish as 'the earliest friend

PURCLEWAN MILL, 1985

except my brother that I have on earth and one of the worthiest fellows that ever any man called by the name of friend.'
Also see: Coylton; Leglen Woods; Newark Castle.

RATTON-KEY   Map Ref. 335 223
A quay of Ayr Harbour, situated in South Harbour Street, opposite Fort Street. It is no longer extant.
It is referred to in the poem *THE BRIGS OF AYR* — '*And from Glenbuck, doon to the Ratton-Key.*' In a note to the poem, Burns indicated that it referred to — 'a small landing place above the large quay.'

RICCARTON
Situated on the B7038 Kilmarnock/Ayr Road, 2 miles south of Kilmarnock town centre.
In the poem *THE VISION*, Sir Adam Wallace of Riccarton is referred to as '*Bold Richardton.*' Sir Adam was a cousin of William Wallace, the Scottish patriot.
The Rev. Alexander Moodie, '*Singet Sawnie*' of the poem *THE TWA HERDS*, was minister of Riccarton Parish Church from 1761 to 1799. He was also referred to in the poem *THE HOLY FAIR* — '*For Moodie speels the holy door.*'
The present church was built in 1823. Rev. Moodie is buried in the kirkyard.

RICHMOND'S HOUSE   Map Ref. 498 274
Situated at No. 3 High Street, Mauchline. The house is still extant. Local tradition maintains that it was the home of John Richmond, close friend and confidant of Burns.
Richmond's father was a merchant in Mauchline and also owned Montgarswood Farm, Mauchline which was for several years farmed by 'Holy Willie' Fisher.
Born in 1765, probably at Montgarswood Farm, Richmond was educated at

High Street, Mauchline, with Richmond's house second from the left
circa 1900

Newmilns school. He started work as a clerk to the poet's friend and patron, Gavin Hamilton, Mauchline. In 1785 he moved to Edinburgh and when Burns paid his first visit to the capital in 1786 he shared Richmond's lodging. About 1789, he returned to Mauchline, married a local girl, Jenny Surgeoner, and set up business as a lawyer.

Jenny Surgeoner had had an illegitimate child by Richmond in 1784, for which they had to appear before the church session and congregation. Richmond would not marry her at that time but did so 6 years later. In a letter dated 1 September 1786, Burns chastised Richmond for his treatment of Jenny.

Burns, Richmond and their friends James Smith and William Hunter formed the bachelor association called the Court of Equity, subject of a bawdy poem of the same name. Burns, Richmond and Smith were together in Poosie Nancie's Inn Mauchline when they saw the riotous scene which inspired Burns to write the poem *LOVE AND LIBERTY*, better known as *THE JOLLY BEGGARS*.

Richmond died in 1846, aged 82 years, and is buried in Mauchline Kirkyard. Also see Elbow Tavern; Mauchline; Mauchline Kirkyard; Montgarswood Farm.

ROBERTLAND HOUSE   Map Ref. 441 471
Situated on the B769 Stewarton/Glasgow Road, a half mile east of Stewarton. The present house was built shortly before 1820.

It was the Ayrshire home of Sir James Hunter Blair, who was referred to in the poem *ELEGY ON THE DEATH OF SIR JAMES HUNTER BLAIR*. Sir James was born James Hunter, son of an Ayr merchant, and added Blair to his name on marriage. He was Lord Provost of Edinburgh from 1784-86 and when Burns paid his first visit to Edinburgh in 1786, Sir James received him and gave his assistance.

The house was owned later by Sir William Cunningham of Robertland and Auchinskeith. Lady Cunningham is thought to have been the 'Mrs C.' referred to by Burns in a letter dated 3 April, 1786 to Robert Aiken, Ayr.

In a letter dated 16 October, 1789 to Captain Riddell, Glenriddell, Dumfries from Ellisland, the poet asked for an enclosed letter to be forwarded to Sir William Cunningham.

Burns visited Robertland and tradition maintains that during a visit the poet confirmed that Douglas Graham was the model for Tam O'Shanter in the poem of that name. When asked about the identity, he is said to have replied — "Tam! It was none else but the guid man of Shanter."

The poet's uncle, Robert Burnes, who lived in Stewarton, may have been Land Steward for Robertland Estate but this cannot be confirmed.

Also see: Auchinskeith; Patie's Mill; Stewarton.

RODGER'S SCHOOL   Map Ref. 239 075

Situated in Main Street, Kirkoswald and now part of the Shanter Hotel. A plaque on the outside wall of the building commemorates the school. In 1775, Burns went from his home at Mount Oliphant Farm, Alloway, to attend the school run by Hugh Rodger for one term — 'to learn Mensuration, Surveying, Dialling, etc.' — to quote the poet.

While attending the school, the poet lodged at Ballochneil Farm and Mill, 2 miles south of the village. The farmer/miller was Robert Niven and the poet's maternal uncle, Samuel Broun was married to Niven's daughter, Margaret. Burns probably lodged with his uncle but he referred to Robert Niven's son, John, as his bedfellow, suggesting that he may have at least slept with the Nivens.

Later in life, Burns claimed that during his time at Kirkoswald, he — 'learned to look unconcernedly on a large tavern bill and to mix without fear in a drunken squabble.' His claim was certainly an exaggeration; a penniless 16 year old lodging 2 miles south of the village would be unlikely to be involved in the circumstances described.

Hugh Rodger's home was on the south side of Kirkbrae, Kirkoswald, which is directly opposite the gate of the old kirkyard. The house is no longer extant.

In Kirkoswald, Burns met his second known sweetheart, Peggy Thomson, a girl of about his own age who lived in the neighbouring house to the school. He went into the back garden of the school house to take measurements and saw Peggy in the garden of her home. He described the meeting — 'stepping out to the garden one charming noon to take the sun's altitude, I met with my angel.'

Amongst his fellow pupils at the school were three members of the Niven family, cousins to each other. John Niven of Ballochneil Farm and Mill was the boy referred to by the poet as his bedfellow; he succeeded his father in the farm and married Jean Rodger, daughter of his old schoolmaster; he was made a Freeman of Maybole for his generosity and benevolence to the people of the town at a time of difficulty. William Niven was the son of a Maybole shopkeeper who also owned Kirklandhill Farm west of the town; he became a very wealthy and avaricious businessman; he was appointed to Maybole Town Council and appointed a Depute Lord Lieutenant of Ayrshire. While they were attending Rodger's School as boys, Burns occasionaly spent his weekend break at William Niven's home in Maybole. Alexander Niven belonged to Girvan; he became a minister; as a student, he was tutor to the children of John Hamilton of Sundrum; in a letter to William Niven from Lochlea, dated 12 June, 1781, Burns wrote — 'Our communion was on Sunday se'en night, I mention this to tell you that I saw your cousin there, with some of Mr Hamilton's sons. You cannot imagine how pleased I was to steal a look at him, and trace the resemblance of my old friend. I was predisposed in favour ... by that ingenuous modesty ... which is so apparent in his manner.' Alexander Niven visited Burns at Mossgiel.

Tradition maintains that Burns and William Niven joined the school on the same day and, as was the custom, they took the schoolmaster to the local inn and treated him to a refreshment. The inn was The Ladies' House immortalised by the poet later as 'The Lord's House' in the poem TAM O' SHANTER.

Another tradition concerning the poet's time at Rodger's school maintains that outwith the classroom, Burns and William Niven, both bright pupils and well-read for country youths, tested each other's mettle in friendly debating jousts on a wide variety of subjects. Mr. Rodger became aware of the contests and looked on their supposed debating skills with contempt. One day, in class, he sneeringly asked what the subject of debate had been for that day and on being told it was whether a great General or a respectable merchant made the greater contribution to society, Rodger laughed derisively. Burns suggested that the master should choose the side of the argument he favoured and he, Burns, would adopt the opposite stance. Rodger chose to support the General and led off the debate in front of the class. It soon became obvious to Rodger and his pupils that Burns was his superior in debating. Pupils recalled later that Rodger had abruptly closed the debate and dismissed the class in a state of agitation at having been defeated.

Also see: Ballochneil Farm and Mill; Kirkoswald; Maybole; Minnybae Farm; Peggy Thomson's House; The Ladies' House.

RONALD'S INN   Map Ref. 498 272
The inn was in Mauchline but little is known about it. Its location has been described as on the south side of Loudoun Street, on the site now occupied by the baker's shop at No. 57.

A Mrs. Alexander of Mauchline, daughter of John Richmond and Jenny Surgeoner, close friends of Burns and Jean Armour, claimed that the poet and Jean were married in Ronald's Inn. Although her information came from her parents it cannot be deemed to be totally accurate as her father was in Edinburgh at the time of the marriage. Although there is no evidence to support Mrs Alexander neither is there evidence to refute the claim.

The inn is sometimes confused with Morton's Inn and Ballroom which was adjacent to Mauchline 'Castle' and is also said to have been the location of the wedding ceremony.

The innkeeper was called John Ronald. A man of the same name operated as the Mauchline/Glasgow carrier and Burns made use of his services. In a letter from Edinburgh dated 17 September, 1787, the poet wrote to his brother Gilbert at Mossgiel — "I am thinking to cause my old mare to meet me, by means of John Ronald, at Glasgow." It is probable that the innkeeper and carrier were the same person.

John Ronald the carrier was the uncle of William Ronald who worked for the poet at Mossgiel and later farmed at Mauleside, Beith.

Also see: Gavin Hamilton's House; Gilmilnscroft House; Mauleside; Morton's Ballroom; Richmond's House.

RYE WATER   Map Ref. 299 499
The river joins the River Garnock from the north, at the Map Reference shown, at the east end of Dalry, Ayrshire.

There has been much speculation as to whether the word 'Rye' of the song Comin Thro' The Rye, refers to the Rye Water or to the cereal crop, rye.

There is nothing recorded by the poet to prove the matter either way. The most significant evidence is that when he submitted the song to Johnson for his Scots Musical Museum, the poet spelled Rye with a small 'r', which indicates that it did not refer to the river.

The song was very old, with several bawdy versions, before Burns improved it.

ST. MARGARET'S HILL   Map Ref. 527 372
The name given by the poet's friend the Rev. Dr. George Lawrie to his home, Loudoun Manse, Newmilns. The house is still occupied though no longer the manse. It is situated at No. 116 Loudoun Road, Newmilns.

In a letter dated 13 November, 1786 to the Rev. Dr. Lawrie, the poet wrote — 'I think the peaceful unity of St. Margaret's Hill can only be excelled by the harmonius concord of Apocalyptic Zion.'

Writing from Edinburgh to Rev. Lawrie on 5 February, 1787, Burns wrote

— 'My compliments to all the happy inmates of St. Margaret's.'

On 15 November, 1788, the poet wrote from Mauchline to the son of the Manse, Archibald Lawrie, later a minister and incumbent of Loudoun Kirk and Manse — 'Please return to me by Connel, the bearer, the two volumes of songs I left last time I was at St. Margaret's.'

Also see: Loudoun Manse.

ST. QUIVOX

A hamlet situated a half mile north of the A758 Ayr/Mauchline Road at Auchincruive, one mile east of the A77 Ayr By-pass.

The Rev. William McQuhae, referred to in the poem *THE TWA HERDS* as — *'That curs'd rascal ca'd McQuhae'* — was minister of St. Quivox from 1764 to 1823. He is buried in the kirkyard.

The church is still extant and used for worship.

The poet's friend, John Tennant, Auchenbay Farm, Ochiltree, later farmed at Shields Farm, St. Quivox, west of the A77 Ayr By-pass.

Also see: Auchenbay Farm.

SHANTER FARM   Map Ref. 218 074

The farm occupied by Douglas Graham, model for Tam O'Shanter in the poem of that name, was not the existing Shanter Farm, Maidens.

The 18th Century farm steading was demolished during the 19th Century. It was situated east of the A719 Ayr/Turnberry Road, a half mile south-east of Maidens village. The house was close to the east side of the disused Ayr/Girvan railway line and near the ancient mote (mound) at the location.

Local tradition maintains that Burns got his inspiration for much of *TAM O' SHANTER* during a visit to Shanter Farm. As a 16 year old, he went from Mount Oliphant to attend Hugh Rodger's school at Kirkoswald and lived at Ballochneil Farm between Kirkoswald and Maidens. According to the tradition, the school's annual summer holiday was on the first Thursday of July, the day of Ayr's annual horse fair. On the holiday, Burns and his school friend John Niven of Ballochneil set out to go fishing at the coast. They went to Maidenhead Bay and embarked on a small boat belonging to Douglas Graham of Shanter Farm and called 'The Tam'. When they were out in the Firth a strong wind got up and threatened to blow them too far out to sea. Niven wanted to return to the shore but Burns refused to do so 'Tho' the wind was blowing strong enough to blaw the horns aff the kye.' At length they returned to the shore and went to Shanter Farm where they were entertained by Douglas Graham's wife, Helen McTaggart. Graham was at Ayr attending the horse fair. Helen was noted for her quick temper and harsh tongue and having expected her husband home early in the evening she became angry when he failed to return. She launched into a tirade of abuse against her husband's character and intemperate habits and prophesied that one day he would fall into the River Doon. In her temper she also spoke against her husband's friend John Davidson the local shoemaker who normally went to Ayr with him and shared his escapades. The tradition concludes with the suggestion that Burns returned to Ballochneil and next morning produced his first draft of the poem *TAM O' SHANTER*.

The story of the fishing trip and visit to Shanter Farm may be based on fact but the drafting of TAM O' SHANTER can only be fantasy. Without doubt the immortal poem was based on an amalgam of such experiences of people and places but it took many more years before the poet produced work even approaching such brilliance.

Also see: Ballochneil Farm and Mill; Glenfoot; Kirkoswald; Laigh Park Farm; Park Farm; Rodger's School; Souter Johnie's House.

SHAWWOOD   Map Ref. 405 260
    The house is still extant as the dwelling-house of Shawwood Farm. It is
situated about a half mile north of the A758 Ayr/Mauchline Road, a half mile east
of Mossblown.
    It was the home of David McLure, a merchant in Ayr. He bought the
property in 1774 and was forced to sell it in 1788 after he had lost money in the
collapse of the Ayr Bank.
    McLure owned Lochlea Farm, Tarbolton and leased it to the poet's father,
William Burnes, in 1777.
    The rent of Lochlea was high and the land poor. The Burnes family worked
hard and lived frugally but were unable to make enough to pay the rent. The
terms of the lease had not been properly recorded and in 1783, after a lengthy
dispute, McLure took out a warrant of sequestration against William Burnes.
Burns defended the action and eventually took his case to the Court of Session,
Edinburgh; the decision was mainly in his favour but by then both his health and
finances were exhausted.
    At one stage of the dispute, John Hamilton of Sundrum Caslte was
appointed referee between the parties. James Grieve, Boghead Farm, Tarbolton,
acted as arbitrator on behalf of McLure and Charles Norval, Gardener, Coilsfield
House in the same capacity for William Burnes. Grieve was the subject of a
satirical mock epitaph.
Also see: Boghead Farm; Coilsfield House; Lochlea Farm; Sundrum Castle.

Ship Inn, Girvan, circa 1890, said to have been visited by Burns

SHIP INN   Map Ref. 186 983
    The inn is no longer extant. It was situated on the west side of Old Street,
Girvan, a short distance south of the wall of the old cemetery.

Burns is reputed to have visited the inn but this cannot be verified. Local tradition maintains that he met the innkeeper's daughter, Nannie Brown, at Kirkdamdie Fair and escorted her home to the inn.

The tradition also maintains that Nannie Brown was the heroine of the song *MY NANIE, O'*, an honour also attributed to amongst others, Agnes Fleming of Coldcothill or Doura Farms, Tarbolton and Agnes McIlwraith of Pinvalley, Barr.

Kirkdamdie Fair was the largest feeing fair of south Ayrshire and was held annually on the last Saturday of May. It was a very ancient fair and was held in the grounds of a ruined church called Kirkdominie on the north bank of the River Stinchar, 1½ miles west of Barr.

Also see: Coldcothill Farm; Doura Farm; Lugar River; Pinvalley; Stinchar River.

Probably the original Simpson's Inn, circa 1890

SIMPSON'S INN   Map Ref. 338 222

The Black Bull public house, River Street, Ayr, close to the north end of the Auld Brig, is, at least on the site of Simpson's Inn; all or part of the existing premises may be the original building but the inn may have been totally replaced about the late 18th or early 19th Century. It has not been possible to prove the history of the inn.

When the poet's father, William Burnes, and other parents, were looking for a school teacher for Alloway, Burnes arranged to meet the 18 year old John Murdoch of Ayr in Simpson's Inn and required Murdoch to produce a sample of his handwriting for examination.

Burns referred to the inn in the poem *THE BRIGS OF AYR* — '*And down by Simpson's wheel'd the left about.*' In a note to the poem he indicated that Simpson's was 'a noted tavern at the Auld Brig end.' The River Street area was then known as Brigend of Ayr.

A letter dated September, 1786 from Burns to John Ballantine, Ayr, accompanying a manuscript copy of the poem *THE BRIGS OF AYR*, was addressed as having been written at 'Simpson's.'

In the legal dispute between William Burnes and his landlord, David McLure, over Lochlea Farm, some of the legal documents were witnessed by John Simpson innkeeper, Brigend of Ayr, which suggests that they were drawn up in the inn.

Also see: Water-Fit.

SMA' INN   Map Ref. 497 274

The Sma' Inn was the name of the establishment commonly known as 'Nance Tannock's.'

Nance Tannock was the maiden name of Mrs Agnes Weir who ran the inn.

Also see: Nance Tannock's Inn.

SMITH'S HOUSE AND SHOP   Map Ref. 498 274

The building which included the house and shop in which the poet's friend, James Smith, lived and worked, was situated at the north side of Mauchline Cross. It was in line with the north sides of Castle Street and High Street, facing on to the Cross.

The building was demolished about 1820 when the new road to Kilmarnock was constructed northwards from the Cross. The road is still known locally as New Road.

The poems *EPISTLE TO JAMES SMITH* and *EPITAPH FOR A WAG IN MAUCHLINE* were addressed to James Smith.

Burns, Smith, John Richmond and William Hunter formed the bachelors' association called *THE COURT OF EQUITY*, referred to in the poem of that name. It should not be confused with Tarbolton Bachelors' Club.

James Smith's sister, Jean, was one of the girls referred to in the poem *THE BELLES OF MAUCHLINE* -- '*Miss Smith she has wit.*' She married the poet's lifelong friend, Doctor James Candlish. The doctor, originally called McCandlish, was born and reared at Purclewan, near Mount Oliphant.

The father of James and Jean Smith died and their mother re-married James Lammie, an elder of Mauchline Kirk. The stepfather was very strict and disapproved of James Smith and his associates.

James Smith eventually emigrated to Jamaica where he died while still young.

Also see: Richmond's House; Purclewan.

SOUTER JOHNIE'S COTTAGE   Map Ref. 240 076

Situated on the east side of the A77 Maybole/Girvan Road in Main Street, Kirkoswald.

The house was occupied from 1785 to his death in 1806 by John Davidson, the prototype of Souter Johnie of the poem *TAM O' SHANTER*. It is now open to the public as a museum.

Davidson and his wife, Ann Gillespie, lived at Glenfoot, Maidens, before they moved to Kirkoswald.

In 1775, Burns attended Hugh Rodger's school at Kirkoswald and lodged at Ballochneil Farm, south of the village. Although he was in Kirkoswald 10 years before the Davidsons moved from Glenfoot, the poet probably knew, or at least knew of, John Davidson, during his stay at Ballochneil.

Also see: Auchenblane; Glenfoot; Kirkoswald; Museums, etc.

SOUTER JOHNIE'S COTTAGE

SOUTH AUCHENBRAIN FARM   Map Ref. 522 305
Situated east of Auchmillan Road, Mauchline, one mile south-west of the
B7037 Galston/Sorn Road.
William Fisher, farmer and kirk elder, referred to by Burns in the poems
HOLY WILLIE'S PRAYER, HOLY WILLIE'S EPITAPH and *THE KIRK'S
ALARM*, lived for most of his life at Montgarswood Farm on the Mauchline/Sorn
Road. Late in life he moved to Tongue Farm, east of the Galston/Sorn Road.
On the evening of 13 February, 1809, aged 72 years, Fisher attended a
meeting in Mauchline and set out in a snowstorm on the 4 miles walk home. At a
part of the road near South Auchenbrain Farm he went off the road, fell into a
ditch and died.
A.B. Todd, Ayrshire poet and antiquarian, who was born at Craighall near
South Auchenbrain gives the following account of Fisher's death in his
Reminiscences Of A Long Life (1906) — "It is a curious fact that in the *EPITAPH
ON HOLY WILLIE*, Burns says of him — 'His soul has ta'en some ither way, I fear
the left-hand road' — and that Fisher, on his way home that night actually took
the left-hand side of a fence and ditch near the farm of Meikle Auchenbrain and
so was drowned, for had he taken the right-hand and proper side he would have
been safe." Todd's father had been one of a party of neighbours who had searched
for and found Fisher. He had also arranged for the body to be taken by horse and
cart to Fisher's home at Tongue and went on ahead to tell the widow.
William Fisher is buried in Mauchline kirkyard.
Also see: Mauchline Kirkyard; Montgarswood Farm.

SPITTALSIDE FARM   Map Ref. 425 277
Situated on the west side of the B730 Tarbolton/Dundonald Road, a half
mile north of Tarbolton Cross.
The poet's friend, David Sillar, was born at Spittalside in 1760 and lived
there until about 1785. The poet corresponded with him and he was addressed in
the two *EPISTLE(S) TO DAVIE*.
Although not a founder member of Tarbolton Bachelors' Club, he joined in
1781. Like Burns, he was a rhymer and after the success of the Kilmarnock

Edition he had a book of mediocre poetry published by John Wilson, Kilmarnock, in 1789. It has probably been more popular for its curiosity value through his connection with Burns than it was when first published.

Sillar also played the fiddle and tried his hand at composing music. In a note to Johnson's Musical Museum, regarding the song A Rosebud By My Early Walk, Burns wrote — 'This air is by David Sillar, quondam merchant, and now a school master, Irvine.'

In Tarbolton, David Sillar worked as a temporary school teacher but the permanent appointment went to John Wilson, previously school master at Craigie. Wilson was immortalised by Burns as 'Doctor Hornbook' in the poem DEATH AND DOCTOR HORNBOOK. Having been unsuccessful in Tarbolton, Sillar started an adventure school at Commonside between Tarbolton and Annbank but it soon failed. He then moved to Irvine where he tried his hand as a shopkeeper but he went bankrupt and landed in the town jail as a debtor. He again became a school teacher, this time in Irvine.

Eventually, Sillar inherited £30,000 or £40,000 and as a properous citizen became a member of Irvine Town Council. In 1826 he became a founder member and first Vice-President of Irvine Burns Club. He died on 2 May, 1830, aged 70 years, and is buried in Irvine Parish kirkyard.

Also see: Commonside; Glasgow Vennel; Irvine; Stair House.

STAIRAIRD   Map Ref. 473 257
Situated on the River Ayr, a half mile south of the A758 Ayr/Mauchline Road, 2 miles west of Mauchline Cross.

It is commonly accepted, though occasionally disputed, that Highland Mary Campbell worked at Coilsfield House, Tarbolton, after leaving the employment of the poet's friend and patron, Gavin Hamilton, Mauchline. It has been suggested that Mary did not work at Coilsfield but at Stairaird Farm which overlooks the River Ayr where it is joined by the Mauchline Burn. Neither of the claims can be substantiated.

Whereas it is generally accepted that the final parting of Burns and Highland Mary Campbell was near Failford, a tradition maintains that the parting was at Stairaird, where the Mauchline Burn joins the River Ayr. A description of the location given by Burns can be applied equally to Stairaird — 'We met by appointment, on the second Sunday of May, in a sequestered spot by the banks of Ayr.' However, the first stanza of the poem HIGHLAND MARY indicates that, as the location nearer to Montgomerie House (Coilsfield), Failford must be favoured — 'Ye banks and braes and streams around, The castle o' Montgomery. For there I took the last Farewell, O' my sweet Highland Mary.'

A wood near Kingencleugh, Mauchline is also said to have been the location of the parting.

Doctor Thomas Armour, a descendant of the Armour family of Mauchline and relation of Jean Armour, occupied Stairaird Farm in the 1890's.

Also see: Coilsfield; Failford; Kingencleugh; Mauchline Burn; Montgomerie House.

STAIR CHURCH   Map Ref. 439 236
The present church was built in 1864 on the site of the original.

Mrs Catherine Stewart of Stair House and Afton Lodge, the poet's early patron, and James Andrew, friend of the poet and miller at Barskimming Mill, are buried in the kirkyard.

Also see: Afton Lodge; Barskimming Mill: Bridge Holm; Stair House.

STAIR HOUSE   Map Ref. 440 238
Situated on the south bank of the River Ayr, 300 yards east of the B730 Tarbolton/Drongan Road at Stair. The house is still occupied.

It was the home of Mrs. Catherine Stewart of Stair and later of Afton Lodge, the first member of the 'gentry' to befriend and encourage the poet.

STAIR HOUSE

Burns and his friend, David Sillar, visited the kitchen of Stair House where Sillar was courting the nurserymaid, Peggy Orr. In the kitchen they were in the company of Peggy and the housekeeper, Mary (Mailly) Crosbie, and Burns was amusing them by singing and reciting some of his compositions. Mrs. Stewart heard the sound of singing and laughing and sent for her housekeeper. On being told that Robin Burns from Mossgiel was the cause of the hilarity, Mrs. Stewart invited him up to the drawing room and thus began a long friendship and patronage.

Peggy Orr was referred to in the poem *(FIRST) EPISTLE TO DAVIE* — *'You hae your Meg, your dearest part, And I my darling Jean.'* Peggy and Davie were engaged, but only briefly.

In Stair Parish, tradition maintains that the poem *FAREWELL TO ELIZA* was written to a servant at Stair House called Betty Campbell. Nothing is known about the girl to support or refute the tradition. It is generally accepted that the poem was addressed to Miss Betty Miller, one of the girls referred to in the poem *THE BELLES OF MAUCHLINE.*

David Sillar eventually moved from Tarbolton Parish to Irvine. He inherited wealth of between £30,000 and £40,000 and was able to lend £4,000 to the daughters of Mrs. Stewart.

Also see: Afton Lodge; Kilwinning; Milton; Stair Church.

STAR INN CLOSE   Map Ref. 429 380
The close is no longer extant. It was on the north side on Waterloo Street, Kilmarnock, a few yards out of The Cross. The site is now under the modern shopping complex called The Kilmarnock Centre.

John Wilson's printing workshop in which the poems of Robert Burns first appeared in print in the Kilmarnock Edition in July, 1786, was in the attic of a 2 storey building entered from Star Inn Close. Six hundred and twelve copies were printed, all of which were sold in just over a month. The employee who actually

STAR INN CLOSE, circa 1920

printed the books and spoke with pride of having done so for the rest of his life was Walter Graham of Kilmarnock.

Tradition maintains that Burns first asked Messrs. Dunlop and Wilson of Glasgow, the West of Scotland's leading printers and booksellers, to print his poems but they declined.

In 1803, Wilson moved to Ayr and, with his brother, Peter, started Ayrshire's first newspaper, The Ayr Advertiser. He died on 6 May, 1821 and was buried in the kirkyard of Kilmarnock High Kirk.

There has been much debate as to whether or not Wilson was the subject of the poem *ON WEE JOHNIE*. A Mauchline bookseller, also called John Wilson was possibly the person to whom the poem referred. The poet gave no indication of the person concerned.

Also see: High Kirk, Kilmarnock; Kilmarnock.

STEVENSTON

Situated on the A78 Irvine/Greenock Road, 5 miles north of Irvine.

Mayville House, No. 31 High Road, was the home of Lesley Baillie, the poet's 'Bonie Lesley'. Miss Baillie was the heroine of the songs *SAW YE BONIE LESLEY* and *BLYTHE HAE I BEEN ON YON HILL*. She was born at Mayville on 6 March, 1768 and died in Edinburgh on 12 July, 1843.

A memorial column erected by Lesley Baillie's father, Robert Baillie, to the memory of his wife and family, stands on the east side of Glencairn Street, alongside No. 110.

Local tradition maintains that Burns visited the Baillie family at Mayville. He did visit them but probably while they were in Edinburgh.

John Lambie, a native of Stevenston who returned there later in life, and worked for Burns as a gaudsman at Mossgiel, claimed to have been leading the plough when Burns turned over the nest of the fieldmouse, which inspired the poem *TO A MOUSE*.

Also see: Mayville; Mossgiel Farm.

STEWART KYLE

The ancient division of Ayrshire called Kyle is sub-divided into King's Kyle and Stewart Kyle. Stewart Kyle is that part of Ayrshire between the Rivers Irvine and Ayr. King's Kyle is the part between the Rivers Ayr and Doon.

Stewart Kyle was referred to in the poem *THE MAUCHLINE LADY* — *'When first I came to Stewart Kyle, My mind it was na steady.'*

Also see: Carrick; Cunninghame; Kyle.

STEWARTON

Situated on the A735 Kilmarnock/Lugton Road, 4 miles north of Kilmarnock.

When the poet's uncle, Robert Burnes, moved to Ayrshire from the east of Scotland, he settled in the Stewarton area. For several years he lived at Titwood, west of the town, and worked at lime quarries at Lochridge. Eventually, he was crippled with arthritis or rheumatism and moved into Stewarton, living first in a house in the Buck's Head Close and later in another house, the location of which is unknown.

Robert Burnes died on 3 January, 1789 and is buried in Stewarton kirkyard. On 9 January, the poet wrote from Ellisland to his cousin, James Burness of Montrose with the news of their uncle's death — 'We have lost poor uncle Robert ...His son, William has been with me this winter, and goes in May to bind himself to be a mason with my father-in-law ...His other son, John comes to me, I expect in summer ...His only daughter, Fanny, Has been with me ever since her father's death.'

On 24 September, 1910 Stewarton Literary Society erected a memorial in Stewarton kirkyard to the poet's uncle Robert and his eldest son, John, who died on 17 February 1846. The memorial, still in good condition, is situated against the boundary fence on the right on entering the main gate of the kirkyard.

Frances (Fanny) Burns married Jean Armour's brother, Adam Armour, builder, Mauchline who was referred to in the poem *ADAM ARMOUR'S PRAYER*. They lived in Mauchline and had 5 sons and 4 daughters.

The poet was familiar with the town and district of Stewarton by visiting his uncle, visiting Robertland House, and passing through on his way to Dunlop House.

It is believed that the poet's *EPIGRAM ON ROUGH ROADS* was composed during his Highland tour.

Also see: Dunlop House; Lochridge; Robertland; Titwood.

STINCHAR RIVER   Map Ref. 079 815

The river flows south-west through Ayrshire and enters the Firth of Clyde in Ballantrae, at the Map Reference shown.

In all editions of his work up to and including 1794, Burns made the first line of the song *MY NANIE, O'* — *'Behind yon hills where Stinchar flows.'*.

In a letter to George Thomson, song collector, in 1792, Burns wrote — 'The name of the river is horribly prosaic. — I will alter it.' He then gave the choice of Girvan and Lugar. Thomson chose Lugar and so it has remained in many editions. Burns also commented in his letter — 'Girvan is the river that suits the idea of the stanza best.'

As Stinchar was the first choice and, of the others, Girvan suited the idea best, it appears that the song was set in south Ayrshire. If the poet composed the song at Mount Oliphant or Kirkoswald, the setting sun would first darken the sky in the east where the Stinchar and Girvan Rivers flow *'Mang moors an' mosses many o'* as described in the first verse of the song.

It is generally accepted that the heroine of the song was Agnes Fleming of Coldcothill or Doura Farms, neighbouring Lochlea. If she was, it is incredible that the poet chose Stinchar or Girvan as suitable for his introduction, as neither of them have any relationship with the sun setting in the west or darkening the eastern sky as seen from Lochlea.

The poet's brother, Gilbert Burns, said that Agnes Fleming was the heroine; his youngest sister, Isabella Burns Begg, said that it was Peggy Thomson of Kirkoswald; the poet's aunt, Mrs. Brown of Kirkoswald said that the heroine was Agnes McIlwraith of Pinvalley; local tradition in Girvan maintains that it was Agnes Brown, daughter of the proprietor of the Ship Inn, Girvan; and Rev. Hamilton Paul, 19th century Burns scholar said that it was an Agnes Sheriff of Kilmarnock. The poet gave no indication of the identity of the heroine of his song. In his First Commonplace Book he commented — 'Whether the following song will stand the test, I will not pretend to say, because it is my own: only I can say it was, at the time, real."

Also see: Coldcothill Farm; Doura Farm; Girvan River; Kirkoswald; Lugar River; Minnybae Farm; Pinvalley; Ship Inn; Stinchar River.

SUN INN   Map Ref. 498 273

The inn is no longer extant. It was probably situated on the south side of Mauchline Cross, in line with the south side of Loudoun Street, and removed when Earl Grey Street was constructed.

It was owned by John Miller whose daughters Elizabeth (Betty) and Helen were two of the girls referred to in the poem *THE BELLES OF MAUCHLINE* — *'Miss Betty is Braw'* and *'Miss Miller is fine.'*

The poet was briefly infatuated with Elizabeth Miller and she was probably the heroine of the poem *FROM THEE ELIZA*, written while he was contemplating departure for the West Indies. She married William Templeton, a Mauchline shopkeeper, and died young in childbirth.

Helen Miller married the poet's friend and physician, Doctor John Mackenzie, who lodged in the Sun Inn until he was married. They moved to Irvine where she died and is buried in the parish kirkyard.

The Miller family were referred to in the poem *A MAUCHLINE WEDDING* which was inspired by the marriage of John Miller's son, William, to a sister of a local man called Alexander Bell who had made a fortune in Jamaica.

Also see: Back Causeway; Irvine; Stair House.

SUNDRUM CASTLE   Map Ref; 411 212

Situated one mile north of the A70 Ayr/Cumnock Road, 1½ miles west of Coylton. The Castle is still extant.

It was the home of John Hamilton, businessman and agricultural improver, who was appointed as referee in the dispute between the poet's father, William Burnes, and his landlord, David McLure, over Lochlea Farm. Hamilton found mainly in favour of Burnes.

In a note to a suppressed stanza of the poem *THE VISION*, Burns indicated that the following lines relate to Sundrum — *'Where hid behind a spreading wood, An ancient pict-built mansion stood.'* The 'female pair' referred to in the stanza were John Hamilton's daughter's Lilias and Margaret.

Also see: Lochlea Farm; Rodger's School.

SYMINGTON

The village is situated on the A77 Ayr/Kilmarnock Road, 4 miles south of Kilmarnock.

The Rev. William Auld, Minister of Mauchline Parish Church when the poet was at Mossgiel Farm, was born at Ellanton (Helenton), Symington. His father was Laird of Ellanton.

The Rev. Auld was referred to as *'Daddy Auld'* in the poem *THE KIRK'S ALARM.* In his introduction to the poem *HOLY WILLIE'S PRAYER,* and in a letter dated December, 1787 to Gavin Hamilton, Mauchline, the poet referred to the minister as *'Father Auld'.*

It was before Rev. Auld, his session and his congregation that Burns and Jean Armour were required to do penance for their illegitimate children.
Also see: Mauchline Kirkyard.

The Cairn — 'Whare hunters fand the murder'd bairn'.

TAM O' SHANTER'S JOURNEY

Armstrong's 1775 map of Ayrshire shows two roads from Ayr to the River Doon and south-west Ayrshire; one route follows the line of the B7024 Ayr/Alloway/Maybole Road and the other the line of the A719 Ayr/Doonfoot/Dunure Road. In addition, Greenfield Avenue, joining the two roads, had been constructed by the poet's father William Burnes in 1755/56.

Although the poem *TAM O'SHANTER* was not composed until 1790, Burns set the poem in a time before the new roads were constructed. Poetic licence also played a part in the account of Tam's route.

Having left the High Street, Ayr by Cow Vennel (Alloway Street) or Carrick Vennel (Carrick Street), Tam —
'Weel mounted on his grey mare Meg'

made his way across the rough common land between the modern Dalblair Road/Alloway Street area and the Curtecan (now Slaphouse) Burn. The burn still flows west under Monument Road, through Belleisle Park and under Doonfoot Road to the sea.

It is not generally realised that some of the important landmarks highlighted by Burns in *TAM O' SHANTER* did exist and that some still do.

Let us take up the story of Tam O' Shanter's journey as he approached Alloway and —

'Kirk-Alloway was drawing nigh,
Where ghaists and houlets nightly cry.'

The route ran parallel to Monument Road, along the east side of Belleisle Park until it reached the Slaphouse Burn —

'By this time he was cross the ford,
Whare in the snaw the chapman smoor'd.

In fact, the burn had been bridged by the mid 17th century but the poet preferred to have Tam ford it. The ford was probably about 100 yards west of Monument Road.

Tam pressed on towards Alloway —

'And past the birks and meikle stane,
Where drunken Charlie brak's neck-bane.'

The meikle stane is no longer extant. It was situated on what is now the east side of Belleisle Park, about 100 yards south of the Monument Road entrance.

The route then veered slightly to the west and passed to the west of Burns Cottage, across the ground now occupied by Wrightfield Nursery, until it went —

'...thro' the whins and by the cairn,
Whare hunters fand the murder'd bairn.'

The ancient cairn was situated on what is now the site of a house in Cairn Crescent, a few hundred yards south-west of Burns Cottage. To allow building development, the cairn was removed from its original site in 1964 and on its removal was found to have covered an ancient burial kist (grave). By arrangement with the building contractor, part of the cairn and stones from the kist were used in 1965 to erect a small commemorative cairn on the north footpath of Cairn Crescent, between numbers 5 x 7 (Map Ref. 329 185), close to the original site.

After the cairn, Tam passed —

'Near the thorn, aboon the well,
Where Mungo's mither hang'd hersel.'

The well still exists at Map Reference 332 181 and is called St. Mungo's Well, supposedly after the patron saint of Alloway. It is situated on the steep north bank of the River Doon, alongside the north end of the disused railway bridge which crosses the river a short distance down-stream from the modern Doon Bridge. To see the unmarked and neglected well, walk down the embankment of the disused railway line which runs parallel to the road leading to the Land o' Burns Centre, go through the runnel under the main road, and as you emerge from the south end of the tunnel look over the west parapet on to the steep north bank of the river. The thorn tree is no longer extant.

There is no local legend of a hanging at the well and we must presume that the poet's licence turned St. Mungo's Well into the place where an imaginary Mungo's mother met her end.

When he had reached the well on the bank of the river, Tam saw —

'Before him Doon pour(s) all his floods'

heard —

'The doubling storm roar(s) thro' the woods'

and was astonished to see that —

'....glimmering thro' the groaning trees,
Kirk-Alloway seem'd in a bleeze.'

Once more poetic licence had taken over. In fact, on Tam's route, the ruined kirk would be reached before the well and the river. When Tam fled from the kirk, pursued by the witches, Meg 'did her speedy utmost' and won 'the key-stane of the brig' to reach safety.

Like Tam O' Shanter in the poem, the account of the journey ends on the old Doon Bridge.

It is strange that the cairn and the well, two of the most widely known features in the works of Burns, indeed in all of English literature, are unmarked and unpublicised within a stone-throw of the Land o' Burns Centre, hub of the Burns Heritage Trail.

The Well — 'Where Mungo's mither hang'd hersel'.

TAM SAMSON'S HOUSE   Map Ref. 432 379

The house is no longer extant. The site is indicated by a plaque on a wall at the south side of London Road, Kilmarnock, at its junction with Braeside Street.

The house was called 'Rosebank' and was almost certainly visited by Burns.

Tam Samson was born in Ochiltree. He was a nurseryman in Kilmarnock, where the firm he founded is still in business. He was the subject of the poems *TAM SAMSON'S ELEGY* and *TAM SAMSON'S EPITAPH*.

Tam Samson was a keen sportsman, especially fond of shooting. One day Burns was in their favourite Kilmarnock tavern, Bowling Green House, which was conducted by Tam's son-in-law, Sandy Patrick. Tam was out shooting and late in returning. His nephew was present and told Burns that Tam had always said that he would be happy to die out shooting on the moors and perhaps his wish had been granted. The poet retired from the company for a short time. By the time Tam returned, Burns was able to read to the company the poem *TAM SAMSON'S ELEGY*. Tam protested that he did not like the story and would prefer the world to know that he was hale and hearty. After a few minutes, Burns restored Tam's confidence and remedied the situation by reading out *TAM SAMSON'S EPITAPH* and its 'per contra.'

Tam Samson died 7 months before Burns and is buried in the Laigh Kirkyard, Kilmarnock. The Epitaph is inscribed on his headstone.

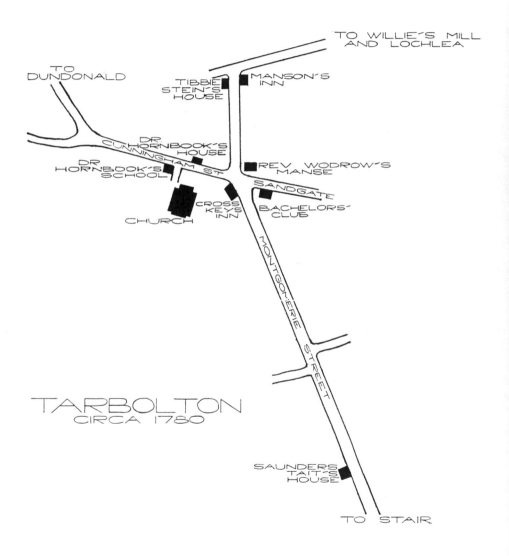

TO WILLIE'S MILL
AND LOCHLEA

TO
DUNDONALD

TIBBIE
STEIN'S
HOUSE

MANSON'S
INN

DR
HORNBOOK'S
HOUSE

CUNNINGHAM ST

DR
HORNBOOK'S
SCHOOL

REV WODROW'S
MANSE

SANDGATE

CROSS
KEYS
INN

BACHELORS'
CLUB

CHURCH

MONTGOMERIE STREET

TARBOLTON
CIRCA 1780

SAUNDERS
TAIT'S
HOUSE

TO STAIR

TAM SAMSON'S HOUSE

When Burns borrowed a horse from George Reid, Barquharrie Farm, Ochiltree for his journey from Mauchline to Edinburgh in 1786, Tam Samson's brother John, borrowed the horse for a journey back to Kilmarnock.
Also see: Bowling Green House; Dalsangan Mill; Kilmarnock; Laigh Kirk; Ochiltree.

TARBOLTON
Situated on the B730 Dundonald/Coylton Road, one mile north of the A758 Ayr/Mauchline Road.
The town is an important centre in the Burns Country and has many important associations with the poet.
Burns moved into Lochlea Farm in Tarbolton Parish in 1777, aged 18 years, and moved out to Mossgiel Farm, Mauchline in 1784. While he was at Lochlea, the village became the centre of his social life; he joined a dancing class, helped to found the Bachelors' Club, and became a freemason. After he left the parish, he retained some of his connections with Tarbolton, especially as Depute Master of Lodge St. James Tarbolton.
His time in the parish was an important period in the development of Burns as a poet. When he moved in he had already composed some poetry and when he left he had begun to show poetic ability of some worth.
The Rev. Dr. Patrick Wodrow was minister of Tarbolton from 1738 to his death in 1793. He was referred to in the poem *THE TWA HERDS* — '*Auld Wodrow lang has hatch'd mischief.*' He is buried in the kirkyard. The present church was built on the site of the original. Rev. Wodrow's Manse stood on the east side of Burns Street, as its junction with Sandgate.
The Rev. John McMath who was addressed in the poem *TO THE REV. JOHN McMATH* was assistant to Rev. Dr. Wodrow in Tarbolton from 1782 to 1791. He supported the poet's friend, Gavin Hamilton of Mauchline, in his dispute with Mauchline kirk session and asked Burns to send him a copy of the poem *HOLY WILLIE'S PRAYER* which relates to the dispute. Although he had been

appointed as Rev. Wodrow's successor in Tarbolton, McMath became a heavy drinker and had to demit office prematurely in 1791, before the death of Rev. Wodrow.

John Wilson, Tarbolton school teacher, immortalised by Burns as '*Doctor Hornbook*' in the poem *DEATH AND DOCTOR HORNBOOK*, was also session clerk of Tarbolton church and secretary of Lodge St. James, Tarbolton.

Alexander 'Saunders' Tait, who wrote and circulated several rhymes attacking Burns and his friend David Sillar, was a bachelor tailor in Tarbolton. The location of his house is in dispute; it has been reliably described as 'originally a small 2-storey cottage, later modernised and partly rebuilt, on the west side of Montgomerie Street, a short distance above the entrance to the school.' Tait published a book of poems in 1790.

James Findlay, a Tarbolton excise officer is thought to have instructed Burns in the subjects required for excise duties. He married Jean Markland, one of the '*BELLES OF MAUCHLINE*' in the poem of that name — '*Miss Miller is fine, Miss Markland's divine.*' Tradition maintains that the couple were introduced by the poet. They moved to Greenock where Jean is buried.

John Lees, a shoemaker in the village, recounted that as a youth he had acted as 'blackfoot' for Burns in his pursuit of local girls. A 'blackfoot' was a go-between or chaperone between a young man and the girl whose acquaintance he wished to make. Lees said that once he had attracted a girl out of her home on the poet's behalf, Burns would say to him — 'Now, Jock, you can gang awa' hame now.'

William 'Souter' Hood, an elder of Tarbolton Church and also a shoemaker was the subject of a mock epitaph by the poet. Burns recorded it in his First Common-Place Books as *EPITAPH ON WM. HOOD, SENR. IN TARBOLTON* and it is sometimes called *EPITAPH ON A CELEBRATED RULING ELDER.*

The many places in the village and parish connected with Burns and his associates are dealt with separately.

Also see: Adamhill Farm; Bachelors' Club; Coilsfield House; Cross Keys Inn; Doctor Hornbook's House and School; Freemasonry (Tarbolton); Johnie Ged's Hole; Langlands Farm; Lochlea Farm; Manson's Inn; Montgomerie House; Spittalside Farm; Tibbie Stein's House; Tarbolton Mill; Willie's Mill.

TARBOLTON MILL   Map Ref. 435 274

Situated south of the B744 Tarbolton/Galston Road, on the eastern edge of Tarbolton village.

In the poem *DEATH AND DOCTOR HORNBOOK*, Burns referred to it as '*Willie's Mill*', after his friend, William Muir, the miller — ' *I was come round about the hill, An' toddlin down on Willie's Mill.*'

Gilbert Burns the poet's brother, referred to it as 'Tarboth' Mill, a local corruption of Tarbolton. He said that Burns was in the habit of meeting 'Montgomerie's Peggy,' the otherwise unknown heroine of the song of that name, at the mill.

Also see: Coilsfield; Tarbolton; Willie's Mill.

THE CELLARS   Map Ref. 216 082

A cottage situated at No. 53 Ardolochan Road, Maidens. It is still occupied and is thought to be the oldest house in the village.

Local tradition maintains that it is called The Cellars because it was originally an ale-house and that Burns visited the house in 1775 while he was living at Ballochneil Farm, Kirkoswald Parish and attending Hugh Rodger's school in Kirkoswald village.

Part of the cottage may have been used as a smiddy (smithy) either at the time of Burns or later. It is sometimes said to have been occupied by John Niven, model for the smith in the poem *TAM O' SHANTER*. It is generally accepted that

Niven's smiddy was at or near Damhouse of Ardlochan, a half mile north of The Cellars.

Also see: Ardlochan; Ballochneil Farm; Damhouse of Ardlochan; Douglaston; Maidens.

Kirkton Jean's House as Kirkoswald Smiddy, circa 1900

THE LADIES' (LEDDIES') HOUSE   Map Ref. 239 075

The house is no longer extant. It was situated on the west side of Main Street, Kirkoswald, a few yards north of the kirkyard. For the last few years of its existence it was a smiddy (smithy).

When Burns was at school in Kirkoswald in 1775, it was an ale house conducted by two sisters, Jean and Anne Kennedy. The sisters were rather refined and conducted their premises likewise, with the result that it was known as The Ladies' House.

In the poem *TAM O' SHANTER*, Burns changed the name to 'The Lord's House', probably to make the line scan properly, and referred to Jean Kennedy as *'Kirkton Jean'* — *'That at the Lord's house, even on Sunday, Thou drank wi' Kirkton Jean till Monday.'*

The name 'Kirkton' was applied throughout Scotland to a 'town' (hamlet or village) with a kirk.

When the poet started at Hugh Rodger's school in the village he did so with William Niven, the son of a Maybole merchant and a nephew of Robert Niven of Ballochneil Farm, Kirkoswald, where Burns was lodging. As was the custom when boys of their age entered a school, Burns and William Niven took Rodger to The Ladies' House and treated him to a draught of ale.

William Niven became a very wealthy businessman and landowner. He was a Bailie, Town Councillor and Depute Lord Lieutenant of Ayrshire, but with a reputation for meanness. Burns and Niven were lifelong friends.

Also see: Kirkoswald; Maybole; Rodger's School.

TIBBIE STEIN'S HOUSE   Map Ref. 431 273
     The house is no longer extant. It was situated on the west side of Burns
Street, Tarbolton, at its junction with Garden Street and directly opposite the site
of Manson's Inn. It was the home of Isabella Steven, known locally as Tibbie
Stein.
     Burns courted Tibbie but she inherited a legacy of £75 and turned her
attention to another, probably more prosperous suitor. Local legend maintains
that one night Burns called at her home and the door was answered by a member
of the household who said that Tibbie was entertaining another gentleman. The
poet left the house and never returned. It was soon afterwards that he wrote the
song *O' TIBBIE, I HAE SEEN THE DAY.*
     Later in her life Tibbie was pleased to acknowledge that she was the heroine
of the song. She married and became a Mrs. Allan.
     The poet's youngest sister, Isabella Burns Begg, said that Tibbie Stein lived
at Littlehill Farm, neighbouring Lochlea. Tibbie has been described as the
daughter of a small farmer so it is possible that she lived at Littlehill before she
moved to Tarbolton.
     Burns was about 18 years old when he wrote the poem. As Mrs. Begg was 12
years younger than the poet, her information can not be regarded as reliable.
Also see: Littlehill Farm: Tarbolton.

TITWOOD FARM   Map Ref. 403 433
     Situated a half mile west of the A735 Kilmaurs/Stewarton Road, one mile
north of Kilmaurs.
     When the poet's uncle, Robert Burnes, moved to Ayrshire from the east of
Scotland he lived at Titwood Farm and worked at lime quarries at Lochridge,
Stewarton.
     The exact site of his home it not known.

TUNNOCH   Map Ref. 308 097
     Situated on the eastern outskirts of Maybole, north of the B7023 Maybole/
Crosshill Road.
     It was the parental home of Captain Matthew Henderson with whom Burns
was acquainted while both were in Edinburgh. Henderson was the subject of the
poem *ELEGY ON CAPTAIN MATTHEW HENDERSON.* The poem was sub-
titled 'A Gentleman who Held the Patent for His honours immediately from
Almighty God.'
     Burns wrote complimentary remarks about Henderson in letters to Professor
Dugald Stewart, Robert Cleghorn and Robert Graham of Fintry.
     The estate, as it was classed in the time of Burns, was then spelled Tannoch.
     Captain Henderson was also Laird of Tannochside in Lanarkshire.

WALLACE TOWER   Map Ref. 338 218
     Situated in High Street, Ayr at its junction with Mill Vennel.
     The present tower was built on the site of the original in 1834. The original
tower was very ancient, the date of building being unknown; in 1673, Ayr Town
Council bought it from the Cathcarts of Corbieston.
     The tower and its clock are referred to in the poem *THE BRIGS OF AYR* --
'And Wallace Tower had sworn the fact was true.'

WATER-FIT
     It is referred to in the poem *THE HOLY FAIR* — *'Peebles, frae the Water-
Fit.'*
     The name Water-Fit referred to Newton-on-Ayr and is descriptive of its
location at the mouth of the River Ayr; it is that part of Ayr north of the river
and was originally a separate parish.

The Rev. Dr. William Peebles was minister of Newton-on-Ayr and clerk to Ayr Presbytery. He moved to Newton in 1778 and remained there until his death on 11 October, 1826. Peebles Street, Newton-on-Ayr commemorates the minister's long association with the parish.

In 1786, in the midst of the controversy in the Church Of Scotland between the 'Auld Licht' (established) and 'New Light' (modern/liberal) approaches to religious beliefs, the Rev. Dr. William McGill of Ayr published a 'New Licht' essay on The Death Of Jesus Christ. He was attacked as a heretic by Peebles, an 'Auld Licht' fanatic. Burns and his father had both held McGill in high regard during their time near Ayr and the poet stepped into the midst of the controversy with his scathing attack on the 'Auld Licht' clergy in his poem THE KIRK'S ALARM.

Peebles thought he had some poetic ability and had published mediocre poems on religious subjects. In the poem THE KIRK'S ALARM, Burns referred to him as 'Poet Willie' and the stanza relating to him is a sarcastic attack on his attempts at poetry.

Peebles disliked Burns, even after the poet's death, and in 1811 published a bombastic, unchristian attack on the growing cult of Burns appreciation in an essay called "Burnsomania — The celebrity of Robert Burns considered in a Discourse addressed to all real Christians of every Denomination." He denounced the poet's work as 'vile scraps of indecent ribaldry.'

Loudoun Street, Mauchline, with Poosie Nancie's and the site of the Whitefoord Arms circa 1920

WHITEFOORD ARMS   Map Ref. 498 273

The inn is no longer extant. The site is indicated by a plaque on the east gable of the building in Loudoun Street, Mauchline, at the west side of its junction with Cowgate.

It was frequented by the poet and his friends and was the meeting place of the bachelor group called THE COURT OF EQUITY referred to in the poem of that name.

The innkeeper was John Dove or Dow, nicknamed Johnie Doo or Johnie Pigeon by Burns. He is referred to in the poem TO GAVIN HAMILTON, ESQ. as 'Paisley John' and is the subject of the poem EPITAPH ON JOHN DOVE, INNKEEPER. In the poem to JOHN KENNEDY, DUMFRIES HOUSE, the inn is referred to in the lines — *'please step to Dow's, And taste sic gear as Johnie brews.'*

Jean Armour's house was situated in Cowgate, behind the Whitefoord Arms, and separated from it by a lane.

WHITEHILL   Map Ref. 364 183

Situated west of the A713 Ayr/Dalmellington Road, at the Asylum Brae. The original house is no longer extant. The name of the property and its modern house have been changed to 'Glenparks'.

In 1778, when he was 39 years of age, Robert Aiken, an Ayr lawyer, purchased what was later described as 'the considerable estate of Whitehill.'

Robert Aiken was one of the poet's best friends. Burns dedicated the poem *THE COTTER'S SATURDAY NIGHT* to him and in the poem *THE KIRK'S ALARM* he was referred to as *'Orator Bob.'* In letters to their mutual friend, John Ballantine, the poet called Aiken 'my first poetic patron' and 'my first kind patron.'

The support and encouragement given by Aiken to the poet is illustrated best by the fact that of the 612 subscriptions for the Kilmarnock Edition, 145 were arranged by Aiken.

Tradition maintains that John Hunter, another Ayr lawyer who later bought Doonholm House, was responsible for drawing Aiken's attention to the poetic genius of Burns. It must be probable that Aiken knew of the poet through his maternal uncle, the Rev. Dr. William Dalrymple, Minister of Ayr Auld Kirk, who baptised Burns and was friendly with the poet and his father. Aiken was cousin of James Dalrymple of Orangefield, another of the poet's patrons.

The poem *EPISTLE TO A YOUNG FRIEND* was addressed to Robert Aiken's son, Andrew Hunter Aiken. Andrew Aiken's eldest son, Peter Freedland Aiken, became a noted Burns scholar and in 1876 produced a book called Memorials of Robert Burns and his Contemporaries.

Robert Aiken had one daughter called Grace who was born on 12 January, 1777 and died on 13 October, 1857. As a girl she delighted in the poet's visit to her home and to listening to him reciting his compositions. In March, 1796, four months before the poet's death she met him in Dumfries and was distressed by his emaciated appearance and obvious ill-health. Her nephew, Peter Freedland Aiken recounted that the poet had said to her — "The fire in me is almost extinguished; I am the shadow of my former self."

Although it cannot be proved, tradition maintains that there was one shadow over the relationship between Burns and Aiken. In 1786 Burns gave Jean Armour a letter in which he either declared them to be married or, at least, promised to marry her. The ultimate fate of this letter is unknown and the exact wording has not been recorded. It appears to have been regarded by Burns as a marriage contract. Jean told her parents that she was pregnant by Burns and showed them the letter. Her father, James Armour, was furious and did not want Jean associated with the poet. According to tradition he took it to Robert Aiken who cut the names of Robert and Jean out of the letter, rendering it valueless as a contract. Burns was both angry and hurt and blamed Jean. As a result of Robert Aiken's involvement there was a temporary coolness between Burns and his friend.

Robert Aiken, who had been born on 23 August, 1739, died in 1807 and is buried in Ayr Auld Kirkyard.

Also see: Ayr Auld Kirk; Orangefield House.

WHITESTONE COTTAGE   Map Ref. 258 107

Situated on the west side of the A719 Ayr/Turnberry Road, about a half mile south of its junction with the B7023 Maybole/Culzean Road. The exact location is indicated by the ruined gable of the cottage in the wood on the west side on the road, 250 yards south of the large lay-by created by road re-alignment south of the B7023 junction.

Tradition maintains that the poet's mother, Agnes Broun, was born in the cottage on 17 May, 1732.

Agnes Broun's parents, Gilbert Broun of Craigenton Farm, Kirkoswald Parish, and Agnes Rennie of Maybole, were married on 7 May, 1731. Gilbert is said to have been employed as a forester on Culzean Estate and on his marriage to have set up home in Whitestone Cottage on the estate.

The family moved to Craigenton Farm when Agnes was an infant.

Also see: Craigenton Farm.

WILLIE'S MILL, circa 1900

WILLIE'S MILL   Map Ref. 435 274

Situated south of the B744 Tarbolton/Galston Road, on the eastern edge of Tarbolton.

It was the home of William Muir, miller, close friend of the poet and his father. In 1788, when Jean Armour's parents put her out of their home for being pregnant by Burns for a second time, she was befriended and given a home by Willie Muir and his wife.

William Muir is the subject of the very complimentary poem *EPITAPH ON WM. MUIR OF TARBOLTON MILL*.

The mill is referred to in the poem *DEATH AND DOCTOR HORNBOOK* — '*I was come round about the hill, An' toddlin down on Willie's Mill.*' The location of the supposed encounter with Death is still easily recognisable from the description; it is indicated by a plaque on the south verge of the Tarbolton/Largie Road, a few yards west of the road leading to Willie's Mill.

As indicated in the title of the *EPITAPH ON WILLIE MUIR*, the proper name of the mill was and still is. Tarbolton Mill.

Gilbert Burns, the poet's brother, said that the poet was in the habit of meeting 'Montgomerie's Peggy', the otherwise unknown heroine of the song of that name, at Tarboth Mill. Tarboth was a local corruption of Tarbolton.

Also see: Tarbolton.

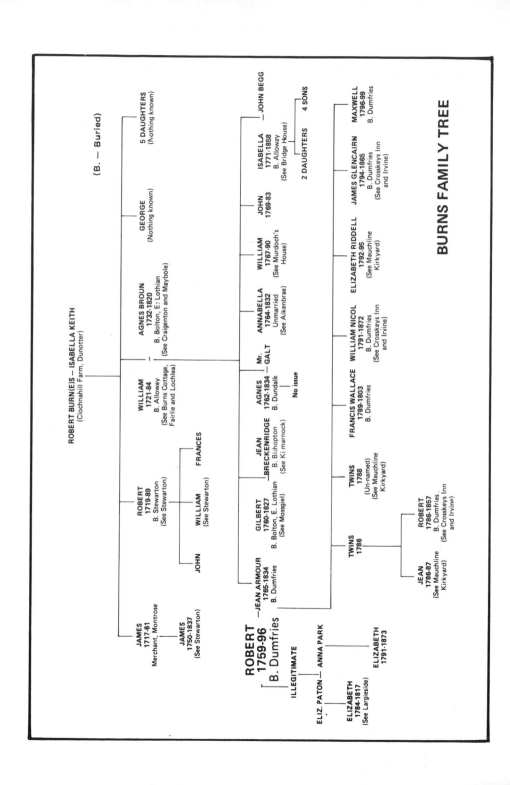

ROBERT BURN(E)S — ISABELLA KEITH
(Clochnahill Farm, Dunotter)

(B. — Buried)

BURNS FAMILY TREE

INDEX OF BURNS'S AYRSHIRE ASSOCIATIONS

'787